The Arthaśāstra Tradition and Ancient Indian Value-System

The Arthaśāstra Tradition and Ancient Indian Value-System

Aparna Mathur

ANAMIKA PUBLISHERS & DISTRIBUTORS (P) LTD
4697/3, 21A, Ansari Road, Daryaganj, New Delhi 110002
Phone: 23281655, 23270239; Fax. : 011-27868035
E-mali : anamikapublishers@yahoo.co.in

First Published 2009

ISBN 978-81-7975-270-8

PRINTED IN INDIA

Published by Anamika Publishers & Distributors (P) Ltd., 4697/3, 21A, Ansari Road, Daryaganj, New Delhi 110002. Typeset by Shivani Computers, Shahadra, Delhi and Printed at Nagri Printers, Delhi.

Contents

Foreword

Though the *Arthaśāstra* of Kauṭilya is the only surviving work of its kind (not to speak of the jejune, cryptic *sūtras* of the *niti*-work that goes by the name of *Bārhaspātya Arthaśāstra*), the tradition of the *śāstra* of *artha* can hardly be gainsaid. Several *arthaśāstrins* and their view were alluded to in the famous work of Kauṭilya and the *Śāntiparvan* of the *Mahābhārata*. Perhaps the unsurpassed treatise of Kauṭilya pushed all of them into oblivion where they were better forgotten and lost like all the grammarians preceding Pānini and his magnum opus, the *Aṣṭādhyāyī*.

A large number of studies on the *Arthaśāstra* of Kauṭilya are already in existence, including a few on *Arthaśāstra* tradition as well but, to my mind, the present work has the distinction of attempting an axiological approach to *Arthaśāstra* tradition in the context of *artha*, which stood for value, as such, before being restricted to material value alone in the scheme of four *purūṣārthas*.

Proceeding from the consideration of value into wider cross-cultural and philosophico-scientific contexts, the study under discussion views the shaping of the concepts of *artha* and the tradition of *arthaśāstra* through the dynamics of historical situations. The challenges brought about in reality were negotiated by practical approaches as well as by the thought processes informing institutional manifestations of society and state both factual as well as normative. Normatively or recommendatorily, they have been visualized in the *arthaśāstra* as well as *dharmaśāstra* traditions.

The study also chronicles the changing notions of the *artha* from the time of the *Ṛgveda* to that of minor law-books and *niti*-works. It also examines its relation with the *arthaśāstra* and at times, *dharmaśāstra* tradition. Finally, the *arthaśāstra* and the *dharmśāastra* scheme of the *purūṣārthas* have been juxtaposed for the comparison.

The study plan of the book, to say the least, is unique. The treatment imparted to it is comparative, well-documented and scholarly. The inferences and conclusions drawn are balanced.

I have every reason to commend this welcome addition to our knowledge in as much as it exposes the more or less taken-for-granted character of *artha* and the *arthaśāstra* tradition are primarily material and political (in the Machiallean sense) respectively to its valuational underponnings mounting it on the immanent value system of ancient Indian culture.

I congratulate the young scholar for giving this important work to the scholarly world.

Prof. OM PRAKASH
Vice Chancellor
M.J.P Rohilkhand University
Bareilly

Introduction

Axiology or science of values is a relatively new and 'not so common' approach in the area of historical research despite the fact that history stands nothing but as Pande defines, 'a process of values-seeking' that culminates finally in the tranformation of this 'seeking' into 'study' and then history may be defined as the study of values. Value, in Indian tradition and literature, has been termed as *artha* that denoted a number of meanings, according to the usages, in the course of its semantic development, yet in all of these meanings, *artha* remained to denote, consistently, as 'meaning' carrying a sense of 'meaningfulness' when attached with something. This brought '*artha*' in the periphery of human attainments for it is only with the reference to the satisfaction of human urge, need or want that the meaningfulness of an object or thing could be ascertained attaching a sense of value to it. *Artha,* therefore, is intimately and inseparably related with human nature which has a five-fold feature as explained in the *Panch-kośa* theory in the *Taittirīya Upaniṣad* providing basis for the development of *artha* to the formation of *purūṣārtha* that leads finally to the '*Paramārtha*' as the ultimate achievement in Indian philosophy of human life. As a study of the development of *artha Arthaśāstra* also has a valuable meaning but in a general sense it is taken as a study of statecraft and political affairs after the Text of Kauṭilya in the same name.

The present work makes a sober and serious attempt to underline the variations in the notion of *artha* and *arthaśāstra* in the course of its historical development with a cultural and axiological perspective of ancient Indian and their philosophy of life. Dr. Aparna Mathur, has done, very successfully, a great but very difficult job, in producing such as scholarly work in this, very important, though not so popular among historians, area of historical study. I am greatly pleased in Introducing Dr. Aparna Mathur and her excellent work to the world of scholars in this field with the confidence that some more high standard works from her pen would make us benefited in future. I wish her best in life.

A.K. Sinha

Preface

Man, among all the living being, is the most evolved creation in this universe and can be distinguished with the other creatures only on the basis of his intellect. A man's life has to possess some meaning beyond existence. Thus, he is the most gifted creation who, under certain parameters, is free to make his own destiny and from this point the question of values arises. He thinks, in a natural way what can be the guiding stars of his life-process because he is a social being and the seeking of values is inherent in his nature and values that he seeks can arise only in the society.

The idea of values, thus, emerges from the idea of man. As in different cultures, the concept of man is different, therefore, the nature of values to be achieved by man also differs. In Indian culture, man is considered primarily as the moral-spiritual being. Therefore, emphasis is laid on those values which helps him in attaining spiritual goals. This emphasis, some times misconceptionally, has been taken as to symbolize the world-negating attitude of the ancient Indians. But in Indian way of life the importance of other material values are also not discarded. Rather, in the form of *Purūṣārtha-Catuṣṭay*, a balanced philosophy of life is developed in which all values essential for man's life, are systematized in a scheme. In this scheme *artha* is included as a material value. But the tradition of *artha* was prevalent in the ancient India from very early period. In this study an attempt has been made to discuss the tradition of *artha* and *arthaśāstra* and its relation with the Indian value-system through the historical study of the concept.

We have adopted an axiological approach which is not much prevalent in historical studies and tried to relate historical changes to the changes that occurred in the ideological sphere, because history of ideas like history of people is a continuous process and with the historical changes, ideas also underwent a change.

This field of study is quite uncommon and without the help and guidance of my revered teacher Prof. Atul Kumar Sinha, Department of Ancient History & Culture, M.J.P. Rohilkhand University, it would have been impossible for me to make any effort in this field. The present study is a result of his active support and efficient guidance. I have no words to express my gratitude to him. The whole credit of this work goes to him only. From my research work to the publication of this book he has motivated and inspired me a lot.

Prof. Om Prakash, the Vice Chancellor, M.J.P. Rohilkhand University, inspires me a lot through his valuable suggestions time to time. Inspite of his busy schedule, he has written the foreword of this book. I am very thankful to him.

I am very grateful to my hon'ble teacher Prof. U.P. Arora, former head of the Department of Ancient History & Culture, M.J.P. Rohilkhand University, Bareilly (now in J.N.U.) for his active support and valuable suggestions that he has given to me. I am equally grateful to Prof. R.P. Yadava, Head, Deptt. of Ancient History & Culture, for the support and suggestions that he has given me time to time during my research work. I am equally indebted to Dr. Abhay Kumar Singh who has been always ready to share and solve my problems. I am also very thankful to Dr. S.B. Lal, and Dr. V.B.S. Yadav, Dr. Anup Ranjan Mishra and Dr. Pankaj

Sharma for the help that they have given me. I am equally thankful to Dr. Rekha Chaturvedi (now in D.D.U. Gorakhpur University) who remains always present to help me at any moment. I am also thankful to Prof. S.N. Kapoor, Head, Department of Ancient Indian History, Culture & Archaeology, Lucknow University who has inspired me time to time. Prof. Samresh Bandhopadhyaya of Kolkata have given mc valuable suggestions for which I am very thankful to him. Prof. O.P. Srivastava of Department of Ancient History, Culture and Archaeology, has given me support and suggestions for which I express my hearty thanks to him.

My all-family members have given me active help in completing my research work. Without their help it would have not been possible for me to complete this work. I am greatly indebted to my parents who never has created any hindrance in my studies and the present work is the result of their love and support. I am greatly indebted to my husband Shri Sanjeev Mathur for the active support that he has given me. In fact the credit of this work goes to him to a large extent. My all sisters have helped me a lot in completing this work; it was only through their efforts that this work received its final shape. I am very thankful to them all. I am greatly indebted to my little daughter Anushka and son Ishan who never created problem for mc. I am also thankful to my friend Dr.Manoj Sharma who is always ready to help me. Thanks to Dr. N.C. Mishra and Dr.Sunil Dixit who have helped me time to time. I am also thankful to the staff of the Central Library of Rohilkhand University for the help that they have given me during my research work. Finally, I am very thankful to Mr. Pankaj Sharma of Anamika Publishers and Distributors (P) Ltd. to bring this book to light.

Aparna Mathur

1. Value and Human Nature

What distinguishes man, as a rational being among all other living beings is his capability to differentiate something from everything or all things depending on his requirements, taste, choice and will.[1] This capability inherent in his original nature develops gradually transforming itself in a sense of value. Thus, promotes man from a mere living individual into a moral, social and finally a cultural being,[2] capable of fulfilling all his likes, wants, and needs and making all his moves and actions meaningful.[3] It is from this original or initial point that the journey of a human culture begins[4] and after crossing the primary stages of its development establishes its identity and individuality in a specific manner on the basis of its different value-system.[5] All cultural developments are, therefore, the development of the value-system and all meaningfulness of a value lies in the satisfaction of the urge, want and need of a person or a human being.[6]

Artha, the primary connotation of value in ancient Indian tradition is, thus, originally attached with the urge, want and need of human person. A thing is *sārthaka* or meaningful only with a reference to the fulfillment and satisfaction of the urge, wants and needs of human being, otherwise it is *nirarthaka*, or meaningless.[7] With the historical development of ancient Indian culture, the word *artha* came to mean different things in different stages yet the primary sense attached to it can never be ignored in all its connotations. This can be seen in a careful historical study of the words *artha* and *arthaśāstra* as is revealed in the following lines.

Keeping an eye over the historical development of ancient Indian culture, we find that the word *arthaśāstra* came to be known as the science of polity and statecraft in ancient India after the famous treatise of Kauṭilya bearing the same title. In his treatise Kauṭilya used *artha* technically in the sense of the livelihood of men and the inhabited land. Therefore, *arthaśāstra* has been termed as the study of the means to acquire, protect and maintain that land.[8] This definition of *artha* transformed it into the politico-economic value and *arthaśāstra* into the science of polity and statecraft.[9] These connotations of *artha* and *arthaśāstra* continued in the later period till the meaning of the words came to stand finally for wealth and science of wealth respectively as these are generally understood.

As in the initial sense *artha* stands for value in general and values can only be understood with a reference to human nature, it would be essential to have an idea of the notion of value and its inherent relation with the nature of man of which values are the basic instincts.

In a dictionary meaning 'value' stands for the worth of a thing in money or goods; estimated worth; purchasing power; that quality of a thing that makes it more or less desirable, useful etc.; the social principles, goals or standard held by an individual, class, society etc.; relative duration, intensity, etc.[10] According to Oxford English Dictionary, "value is worth, utility, desirability and qualities on which these depends."[11] The Cambridge Dictionary of Philosophy defines "value as the worth of something."[12] According to International Encyclopedia of Social Science, "the term 'value' may refer to interests, pleasures, likes, preferences, duties, moral obligations, desires, wants, needs, aversions and attractions and many other modalities of selective orientations. Values in other words, are found in the large and diverse universe of selective behaviour."[13] There is no unanimity among the scholars regarding the definition of the term 'value'. In philosophical as well as in general context, it lacks universal definition. It has been interpreted in a number of different ways. "In general value has been defined in terms of many concepts: value as utility, value as pleasure, value as interest, value as an intrinsic good." [14] Although in the dictionary meaning value primarily meant the worth of something in use and worth in exchange but it was used in a transcendental sense by the Neo-Fictean philosophers. R.B. Perry holds that value possessed "an exalted dignity transcending both nature and sense perception."[15] So value is used in a transcendental sense in philosophy and in the technical meaning in economics.

The notion of value is, generally, grasped through the utility principle that indicates the economic origin of notion. In its dictionary meaning also value is originally meant the worth of something chiefly in economic sense of exchange value. Value- in-use and value-in-exchange are two different senses which are used in economics for the notion of value.[16] Value-in-use refers to the capacity of an object to satisfy human wants and needs and gives rise to the principle of Utilitarianism which is based on the principle of usefulness of a commodity or its power of satisfying human wants or needs. Mill, Sidgewick, Bentham, etc. are the modern thinkers of Utilitarianism but their doctrine doesn't regard utility as an economic notion. Utilitarianism of these thinkers is known as *Universal Ethical Hedonism*, which is based "on the principle of determining moral worth of an action according to the pleasurable consequences." According to this notion an object or a commodity possesses value because it can be useful in satisfying human need or desire. Through the satisfaction of desire or need it evokes a feeling of pleasure that may be termed as value.[17] The Utilitarianism of Mill is based on the psychological concept of desire. He defines value in terms of desire and discovers that pleasure is the only thing desired by human being. He holds,"that which itself valuable is itself desirable." He argues that we, as a matter of fact, desire pleasure, or pleasure is the only object of desire Therefore, pleasure is desirable.[18] But this view of Mill doesn't seem to be correct as he commits a fallacy by assuming 'desired' to mean 'desirable'. Desirable is not desired but it might what ought to be desired. If a thing is not desired for pleasure then it doesn't mean that the thing have no value.[19] Therefore, this doctrine of universal ethical hedonism cannot be accepted fully as it depends on pleasurable consequences of a moral action. Pleasure is a psychological concept and cannot be measured. Secondly, if a moral action gives us no pleasure it doesn't mean that it is of no use or possesses no value.

In Indian system of thought also this notion has its parallels. Indian thinkers also define value by the way of desire and pleasure. Value, i.e. *artha*, has been defined by the *Mīmāṁsakas*[20] "as worthy of being desired."[21] The satisfaction of desire resulting in pleasure or pain constitute the essence of value, i.e. *artha* which is positive or negative depending upon whether pleasure or pain is greater.[22] Vātsyāyana refers value, i.e. *kāma* to worthy of desire and its satisfaction gives pleasure to man.[23] Cārvākas holds that both these notions of *artha* and *kāma* are values.[24] According to them these are the only values of life desired by a man because they give pleasure and satisfaction. This view holds that the ultimate desire of a human being is to achieve pleasure and the efforts of a person should be directed towards the achievement of pleasure and the removal of pain. This is a purely hedonistic view and defines value in term of psychological concept of desire and pleasure, as the followers of utilitarianism did.

R.B. Perry also gives a psychological definition of value, when he defines value in terms of interest. According to him, "a thing-anything has value or is valuable in the original and generic sense when it is the object of an interest-any interest. Or whatever is object of interest is ipso facto valuable."[25] This implies that value is "an object of interest of someone", for it emanates from the 'peculiar relation between the interest and its object' so 'value is the special character of an object which consist in the fact that interest is taken in it'.[26]

G.E. Moore discarded all these definitions, which defines value in terms of some psychological concepts like desire, interest, pleasure, etc. as all these definitions presuppose the fact that the fulfillment of desire, interest is good and gives satisfaction.[27] Moore holds that all these theories define value in terms of something which is not value thus commit a naturalistic fallacy.[28] He says that 'good' refers to a simple, non-natural, unanalysable property like "yellow". Thus, he concludes that notion of good is indefinable and so value is also an indefinable predicate.[29]

A.C. Ewing tries to define 'good' in metaphysical terms by relating it to God. Ewing is of view that ethical concepts can be understood with reference to God.[30] Here also he tries to define "value in terms of supernatural element and the goodness of that element is presupposed" as in previous theories satisfaction and pleasure achieved through fulfillment of desire is presupposed. Therefore, this definition also commits the same fallacy and does not present any satisfactory answer to the problem of definition of value.[31] The notion of value cannot be defined in terms of non-value notions.[32] All such definitions commit the same fallacy.

Nicoloi Hartmann tries to answer this problem through defining value in terms of a value notion. He defines 'value as essence'.[33] Hartmann holds that value is a unique, ultimate and underivable concept which has its own essence and being.[34]

The above discussion clearly reveals that scholars have no unanimity among themselves regarding the notion of value. If definition of value is to be given strictly according to logical rules, the idea of value perhaps cannot be defined for it is a simple notion, the genus of which does not exist.[35] In spite of all these hurdles for purpose of understanding its real connotation, it is quite necessary to define it. The definition of the term 'value' given by Urban is quite nearer to the problem. Urban gives the definition of value by describing the notion of value. According to him value is that which satisfy human needs, wants and helps in the protection of an individual and his race. He concludes that is valuable instrumentally and absolutely, which takes us towards the development of soul and self-realization.[36] This definition of value given by Urban clearly shows that value have no value if it can't save or protect the human being and does not lead him on the path of self-realization.

Values are meaningful for man only and can be understood only with reference to human nature.[37] As the human nature plays an important role in the conception of value, scholars have no unanimity regarding its conception. Different scholars have tried to define the notion of value from different points of view.[38] Values, in fact, are the natural instincts of human nature that can be realized, at the different level of human consciousness from the satisfaction achieved through the fulfillment of some urge, want, desire, etc. Pande holds that "values are the object of valuing a fundamental human activity".[39] As all human activities are reflections of his ideas originating from certain level of consciousness expressed in human nature, values became the subject-matter of human nature. Values have no values if they do not serve the purpose of human urge. Human nature exists at many levels from biological to purely spiritual seeking satisfaction by fulfilling his urge at each level of consciousness.[40] In an attempt of defining the term 'value' one can't ignore the fact that values can be valuated only with reference to human nature.[41] The followers of scientific approach of study, though, attempts to define value from objective point of view[42] but in its primary form, value can be understood only with reference to man.[43] Any attempt[44] of studying the notion of value, through using an objective or scientific approach will not help us in understanding the notion clearly, unless, the reference is made to human nature.[45] The scientific study depends on facts and primarily value is not fact, though, in practice it manifests itself through facts.[46]

For the study of value one has to keep in mind that values are meaningful only for human person. So all values, in a significant sense, are human values.[47] Human being is the only living creature on this earth capable to desire and achieve satisfaction through fulfilling these desires. Like other living beings, man does have requirements for biological necessities, essential for his survival. The difference is that while other living creatures live only for satisfying these necessities, and no higher level of desires can be expected from them, it has given a low place in human life.[48] Man after satisfying his requirements at this primary level of life, makes attempts to move further and trics to achieve new and higher levels of consciousness, with the help of his intelligence. This intelligence of man is the only quality that differentiates him from other living beings.[49] His this quality, through liberating his consciousness from the narrow limit of biological consciousness, expands his vision and inspires him to proceed further and further in search of the infinite, eternal.[50] One can, for instance, notice all these stages of value-consciousness in the life span of a man from his birth to the old age. When a child takes birth his only requirement is the satisfaction of his hunger, the primary necessity for his survival. But as he grows up and cross this primary level of life, he tries to know about many new things, that he looks around him, gains knowledge about other things and proceeds from lower level to higher level of consciousness. This process of gaining knowledge about different things and achieving new and higher level of consciousness through that knowledge, remains continued in his whole life. After gaining the knowledge of the world and fulfilling the duties ascribed to him as a member of family and society in all the other stages of life, in the last stage, he tries to know about the ultimate reality, through controlling his senses and finally reaches to the conclusion that the ultimate reality is nothing but the self-realization. Thus, the process of knowing the world, and its things that begins with the birth of a child finally culminates in the self-realization and the process of knowing world becomes the process of knowing, nothing else, but oneself.[51]

So in human nature a queering instinct is inherent, that always inspires and insists man to explore new and higher level of consciousness. This instinct is nothing but value consciousness.[52] The satisfaction that a human person realized on these different levels of consciousness which inspires him to achieve higher good from the lower, can be termed as value.[53] This process of realizing values remains continued in the whole life of a human being till he attains the highest value. So value and value consciousness both are the matters of the human nature. As different cultures hold diverse views regarding the notion of man and his nature, therefore, the notion of value differs in different cultures. In the ancient Greek culture, the notion of man was defined variously from natural being to political being, while on the other hand in ancient India the man is thought to be a conscious being who, through using his intellect, establishes his superiority over other living beings.[54] This intellect of man in the form of '*dharma*' not only uplifts him above the biological level,[55] but also enhances him towards that the enlightment which is the ultimate end of his life,[56] and the whole meaningfulness of his life lies in attaining the highest goal.[57] Between the lowest and the highest level of consciousness, there are certain other levels also which can be better understood with reference to the *Pañcakośa* theory of the *Taittīrya Upaniṣad*.[58] This theory describes the five *kośa* or levels of consciousness in its process of giving the description of '*Brahman*', the highest reality. The theory begins with the description of the primary level of survival where food looks like *Brahman* (*anna ve Brahman*) and concludes in the final stage of eternal bliss, *satcidānanda*. After attaining it, nothing remains to be unknown. According to Indian seers man has an innate urge to be, to know and to enjoy. These are described as *sat*, *cit* and *ānanda* aspects of man's personality. The highest level of this doctrine is nothing, but the stage of self-realization where man realizes that Ultimate resides nowhere but inside him. This doctrine describes the development of human consciousness at five distinct levels from primary to ultimate. Thus, justifying the Upaniṣadic dictuṃ "*sarvam khalvidam Brahman*", i.e. everything is *Brahman*. This theory of *Taittirīya Upaniṣad* can be taken as an example for understanding the notion of values in relation to human nature.

Undoubtedly, it is the consciousness of intellect or '*dharma*'[59] that differentiates man from other living beings,[60] otherwise on the primary level he has no distinction, other than form and feature.[61] On this primary level the whole consciousness of man is directed towards the fulfillment of these biological necessities and his all values consciousness depends on the fulfillment of these desires.[62] This is the lowest level of human life and constitutes the first level of *Pañca kośa* theory, namely *Annameya kośa*. At this level food looks like *Brahman* because food is undoubtedly the first condition for survival. Thus, on this lowest level food being the ultimate value to be achieved and because for the *Upaniṣads* ultimate desirable value is *Brahman*, hence *anna is Brahman* ('अन्न वै ब्रह्मा').[63] Food is, undoubtedly, the first condition for survival, but it is not the only condition. There are certain other things essentially necessary for the survival that is felt to be needed at the second stage of consciousness, which *Upaniṣads* terms as the *Prāṇameya kośa*. All desirability at this level of consciousness constitutes the next advanced stage of valuation and the value lies in the will to live.

The philosophical and theoretical conception of value, perhaps, will refuse to accept the value achieve at this level as value because there is no freedom of choice which is regarded as the basic pre-requisite for accepting value as a 'value'.[64] All values at these levels are the values under mere compulsion and value in real terms is beyond all compulsions.[65] Valuing, as Pande writes, implies "seeking, choosing, approving".[66] At this stage man neither can seek nor can approve or choose anything. Here the question of value is related to the question of survival that is most important, for no value is valuable for a dead man. Any talk of value is meaningful only for a living man.[67] The consciousness arising at this level, thus, cannot be regarded as the real value consciousness but as it is related to the most important aspect of human life, it cannot be kept out of primary sphere of value.

The real value-consciousness begins from the next level of human consciousness, where the question of choice replaces the question of survival, enabling or inspiring man to act according to his free will.[68] For instance, a person, dying of hunger, will eat any type of food for the sake of his existence but if a person will have fruits, bread and non-veg for satisfying his hunger, then what he should eat, will depend on his taste and desire. So the role of free-will is essential in value.[69] Man uses his emotions and intelligence for choosing between right and wrong, fair and unfair. This level of consciousness corresponds with the third level of

Pañca kośa theory, namely *Manomaya kośa*. Man's intelligence is the quality that assigns him a distinguishing place among other living beings and this intellect through expanding the limits of his personality makes him aware of himself and the world around him, thus turns him into a thoughtful being, which is the foremost quality of a human being.[70] At this stage he realizes the importance of adjustment and sacrifice in life and these appears to be the basic cause for the development of the social instincts of man making the formation of a society possible.[71] Society is important for the human life because as Aristotle said a "man without a society is either a beast or god..." Now the value-consciousness of a man develops in the form of those values, which help in the development of the social aspect of his personality. The feeling of the social welfare replaces the instinct of the free will depending on one's personal taste; will or desire and values of social importance became the dominating factor in one's personality.[72]

Now with the help of intelligence and knowledge gained, man tries to explore new and higher level of self-consciousness that can be equated with the next stage of the *Pañca kośa* theory, namely *Jñānameya kośa*. At this level the process of value-seeking becomes a conscious process, which in the view of Nikam is the first condition for the real conception of value.[73] In other words, value in real terms, can be regarded as value when it is chosen with the help of intellect without any pressure of necessity, restriction, compulsion or prohibition. A man, by nature is a combination of tendencies of good and evil. But he himself remains fully unaware in this regard and lives a life of a being regulated by his natural impulses, until he attains the self-knowledge of a certain level. This dualism of his nature can be traced at different level of his consciousness. He knows about this dualism when he becomes aware of himself. The natural goodness, inherent in human nature, on the one hand, cultivates the ideas of creativity in him and thus helps in the development of his personality through cultivating moral virtues, while on the other hand, the tendencies of evil, inherent in his nature takes him in the opposite direction. The power of 'good' accompanied by knowledge transforms the moral virtues into the social virtues and it is expected from every thoughtful person that he will follow these virtues. But the tendency of evil is also inherent in his nature. Therefore, there may be some occasions where personal good dominates the social goods, then a medium is required that can established social goods after suppressing the evil tendencies. This requirement brings state in existence.[74] Society, thus, leads towards the development of state. In Greek philosophy the development of state is regarded as the *summum bonum*[75] but as Zimmer points out in Indian context, it is not the highest value rather it is regarded as 'means' to achieve the highest value '*moksa*'.[76] Through this conscious process of seeking values human consciousness creates a world of different values that are in full consonance with human nature and reaches at last on that level which is the highest level of human intellect as well as of human nature.[77] This is the final stage in the process of value-consciousness inherent in man and after attaining this level no dualism remains and man attains a stage of eternal bliss and peace.[78] This stage is described as *Ānandameya kośa* in the *Pañca kośa* theory. It is the stage of self-realization.[79] In Indian culture it is the ultimate stage, which is termed as *mokṣa, nirvāna, kaivalya*, etc. in philosophical terminology.[80] At this stage all dualism of joy-sorrow, profit-loss, victory-defeat, friend-enemy, self-other, etc. vanishes and a perfect situation of eternal bliss, *satcitānanda*[81] comes forward in the form of highest value.[82] We can thus, conclude that value-consciousness is that unsatisfied natural consciousness, inherent in human nature, which through suggesting man that satisfaction and pleasure exists no where, as Pande views, inspires him for the searching *bhumā*[83] and satisfy only after attaining that highest level.

The notion of values in Indian system of thoughts, thus, can understand only through keeping this point in view. In Indian culture man is defined, as a moral-spiritual being whose ultimate end is to attain the transcendental ideal.[84] But it is not regarded as a theoretical conception only rather it is expected from an Indian individual that through using other means of life, he will try to attain this highest level in practice also. Therefore, theory and practice are combined in a wonderful way[85] and this conception comes before us in the form of *Purūṣārtha-Catuṣṭay* that is a unique co-ordination of values that can be practically performed for achieving the highest objective. In this system of *purūṣārtha* four different values, related to the different aspects of human life are coordinated in such a way, that they represent the true nature of Indian value-system. Though Hiriyana used the words *Iṣta* and *dvṣta* for value and disvalue respectively. The object of liking is *Iṣta* hence value whatever is avoided, shunned is *dvṣta*, disvalue.[86] But as in these terms the idea of liking and disliking is prominent, therefore, they reflected only the utilitarian conception of value. They lacked that idea of good that is essential to make a value, value. *Artha was the term* that was used in ancient India to denote the idea of value. Yāska used it for value. It can be regarded as equivalent to value because if on one hand it has desirability which is the primary characteristic of a value. On the other hand, it also possesses the idea of good in the form of *purūṣārtha*, which gives *artha* meaning and makes it a value.[87] Thus, *artha* in ancient India stood for value and *arthaśāstra* was the science of value. With the development of the conception of *Purūṣārtha-Catuṣṭaya*, *artha* was included in it in the form of politico-economic value and thereafter it was used mainly in this sense only.

How this broader notion shrinked into a much narrow concept, can be known only after keeping an eye over the development that have occurred in the socio-cultural economic, political and ideological sphere of India. Therefore, for, discussing the concept of values in ancient Indian culture it is essential to have an acquaintance with the social, economic, cultural and political traditions that were prevailed in the country because value can be manifested only with reference to fact that is why for knowing its conception in any particular culture, it is necessary to have a knowledge of the cultural tradition of that country. The earliest period of Indian history was the period of Harrapan culture. In the light of archaeological evidences, there left no doubt about the antiquity of this culture. But as its script is not deciphered yet therefore we cannot assert anything with certainty about the cultural traditions that were prevalent in that period. Therefore, the earliest references of the Indian culture and value-system can be traced only in the early Vedic society.

The only source of knowledge about the early Vedic period is the *Ṛgveda*.[88] In this period, the political expansion of Aryans was limited to the northwestern India. The word '*sapt-sandhav*' is used in this Veda to denote a certain area in which they were living. In this period the culture and society of the Aryans were in rudimentary form. *Jana* was the highest political unit[89] and monarchy was the most prevalent form of government.[90] The whole subject matter of this Veda is available in the forms of hymns that depict a world affirmative attitude of early Vedic people towards life and its problems.[91]

The sources of information about later Vedic age (1000 B.C. to 600 B.C.) are three *Vedas* (*Yajurveda*, *Sāmaveda* and *Atharvaveda*), *Brāhmaṇ* texts, *Upaniṣads*, *Vedangas*, etc. In this period the political supremacy of Aryans was extended up to the Ganga-Yamuna valley. The tribal phase of early age came to an end and these texts reflect the development of a well-developed rural urban civilization. In this age, on the one hand agriculture and industries were developed to a large extent. On the other hand, imperialistic tendencies also grew as a result of which small *janas* of early Vedic age were transformed into big *janapadas.*[92] In the 6th century B.C., we find references to at least sixteen big *janapadas* that arose in northern India.[93]

The contemporary social structure was also not remained unaffected. The *Varṇa-Vyvasthā*[94] or class structure which was founded on the basis of division of labour in the early age, was transformed into complex system. Due to the prevalence of highly ritualistic sacrificial culture the social prestige of the *Brāhmaṇs* was enhanced greatly and they were assigned the highest place in the social system. But this supremacy of *Brāhmaṇs* did not remain unchallenged and various passages of later Vedic literature reflect that *kṣatriyas*, being the ruling class, desired to achieve this privileged.

For the development of the personality of an individual the idea of *āsrama* system was developed in the later Vedic age in which through dividing the whole life span of a man is four stages, namely *Brahmacarya*, *Garhastha*, *Vānaprastha* and *Saṁyas*, an attempt has been made to develop the personality of individual in the totality.[95] In this system man through performing his duties, assigned to him according to his place in social structure, also tries to control his will, desires, and tries to attain *mokṣa*.

This system of *āsramas* appears to be related inseparably to the system of *purūṣārtha*. It can be assumed that for practical achievement of *purūṣārtha*, this system might be developed. Thus, it can be concluded safely that the theoretical conception of *Purūṣārtha-Catuṣṭay* might also developed in the last phase of later Vedic age when the human desires achieve perfection due to the development of idea of *mokṣa* in the *Upaniṣadic* period. In practice, *āsramas* are the means for achieving the values of *purūṣārtha*. In the first *āsrama*, man gains the value of *dharma*. In the second stage i.e., *Grahastha āsarma* he used the knowledge of *dharma* for achieving *artha* and *kāma*, i.e. material possessions and satisfaction that a man gets through satisfying his material desires, and in the last two stages, namely *Vānaprastha* and *Saṁyas*, he left his duties as house holder and tries to control his senses, and makes efforts for the attainment of *mokṣa*. Thus, *purūṣārthas* can be practically achieved through the system of *āsramas*.

In the later Vedic age *Upaniṣads* gave birth to a new philosophy of life and as a result of it old system of sacrifices, which till then became very expensive and ritualistic, began to loose its significance. As imperialism was developed up to this age and *kṣatriyas* as ruler became very powerful therefore they challenged the supremacy of the *Brāhmaṇs*. This age witnessed the growth of various religious and philosophical movements that discarded the superiority of *Brāhmaṇs* and *Yajñas* and suggested easier path for solving problems of life.[96] Among these movements Jainism and Buddhism were most prominent. The foundation of a new urban economy was also laid in this period. Thus in the sixth century B.C., the rise of Magadha was an important event from the political point of view and the rise of Jainism and Buddhism from religious point of view.

This Magdhan Empire was founded by Bimbisāra and was extended by Ajātaśatru through the policies of war and matrimonial relations. After them Śiśunāga dynasty and Nanda dynasty ruled over Magadha. After defeating the last ruler of Nanda dynasty, Dhananada, Chandra Gupta Maurya laid the foundation of Mauryan Empire in four century B.C. Before the foundation of this empire, northwestern boundaries of India also witnessed the invasion of foreigners such as Greeks under the dynamic leadership of Alexander and Persians under Darius. As a result of these invasions, the cultural contacts of India was established with the countries of Europe and Western Asia through water and land routes.[97]

The rise of Mauryan Empire in the fourth century B.C., is an important event of Indian history. This empire gave new dimensions to the imperialistic policy of Magadha. Owing to the unification of country under a single rule, a sound system of administration was also developed. The *Arthaśāstra* of Kauṭilya was an important source of information for this age though there is a big controversy over its date that will be discussed later on.

After Mauryas, Sungas and Kaṇavas ruled over India. Śunga rulers were Brāhmaṇs and this age witnessed the revival of Brahmanism and development of *Sanskrit* language. This age had also witnessed major changes in social sphere. *Manusmṛti* was written in this age. In this age many foreign races such as Indo-Greeks, śakas, Kuṣāṇas, etc. were attacking continuously on the northwestern areas of India. Among these foreign invaders Kuṣāṇas were important and founded a strong empire in India which was extended to a large area. These rulers accepted the Indian culture and religion and Indian culture, art and religion was developed greatly under their rule.

After the downfall of Kuṣāṇa empire India witnessed nearly the two hundred years of political confusion and anarchy which was again ended after the establishment of imperial Gupta empire. The rulers of this dynasty, once again gave India the political unity and all the aspects of Indian culture witnessed an all round development in this age.[98] After the downfall of this Gupta empire in the sixth century A.D., northern India was once again divided into small states among which later Guptas, Maukheries, and Vardhan dynasty were important. Harsavardhan of Vardhan dynasty once again tried to unite India under a single rule but was not succeeded in his attempts as Pulakesin II of Chalukya dynasty in south India destroyed his imperialistic ambitions.

After the downfall of Harsvardhan, feudalistic tendencies that were already set in motion was accelerated. The age from seven to twelve century A.D. is known in India history as Rajput age or as early medieval age. This age witnessed the growth of feudalism. As there was no strong central power in the country, India faced a series of foreign invasions in which attack of Arabs (7-8th Century A.D.) and Turkish Muslims (11th-12th A.D.) were most important. The attack of Arabs was not much significant, as it remained confined to sindh only. But attacks of Turkish Muslim rulers like Mahmud Gaznavi and Mohammed Gori influenced the political atmosphere of the country to a large extent. Mohd. Gori conquered the throne of Delhi and through making Kutub-udin Aibek, his governor, led the foundation of first Muslim empire in India. These Muslim attacks led deep influence on all aspects of Indian life and culture and socio-economic system also changed and some new traditions were developed in it, but importance of older system did not decline. So in short these were the different stages that ancient India witnessed from earliest period. For the knowledge of cultural traditions it is essential to have knowledge of historical development. Without having a knowledge of the historical chronology one cannot understood the changes that occurred in the cultural tradition of a country because changes in historical course certainly but influence on cultural changes which in turn influences the values of life.

As value is not a term, concept or element rather it is a tradition and can be understood only with reference to its tradition. *Artha* in Indian value system is such a term, which can be understood only with reference to its tradition. The word *artha* in ancient India was used for denoting value and it possessed in itself both the elements of valuation, viz.

idea and fact. Therefore, it can be accepted as a synonymous for value. The tradition of *arthaśāstra* in ancient Indian value system is a tradition of values that later on merged into the notion of *purūṣārtha* which in the later age became the sole representative of Indian value system.

In this study an attempt will be made to discuss relation of *artha* and *arthaśāstra* with value, thus, both the terms will be discussed in the axiological way through keeping a close eye on the development of history and culture because value can be understood only with reference to fact. In the present study the connotations of *artha* and *arthaśāstra* will be discussed with reference to human nature which is the first condition of a value for being a value. In this study through narrating-analyzing the tradition of *arthaśāstra* in historical perspective, an eye has been kept on the changes that have been occurred in the tradition due to the actions and reactions of different political, economic, social, religious, moral and psychological factors. Tradition essentially keeps an idea of historicity in itself and in 'history' one cannot discard description. Owing to this the research methodology adopted in this study, is descriptive but there is a logical presentation in the explanation of facts. We have tried best to leave the unimportant description. Analytical method has been adopted for the factual investigation of collected source material. The analytical study of the source material and their historical explanation is the distinctive feature of the methodology adopted. History in itself is a reconstruction of past, therefore, adopted methodology can be termed as analytical reconstruction methodology. History, though, is the study of past, but it equally useful for present and future and this usefulness of history establishes the valuation of the study of history.

NOTES AND REFERENCES

1. Hiriyana, M., *Indian Conception of Values*, Mysore, 1975, p.5; Pande, G.C., *Mulya Mimamsa*, Jaipur, 1973, pp.74-75; cf, Radhakrishnan S., *An Idealist View of life*, (reprint) Delhi, 1979, p.208.
2. Radhakrishnan, S., *op. cit.*, p.208.
3. Sinha, A.K., Mulya Kei Avadharna Aur Swaroop, in *Journal of Ganga Nath Jha Kendriya Sanskrit Vidyapeetha*, Allahabad, p.182.
4. Mukherjee, Radha, Kamal, *The Destiny of Civilization*, Bombay, 1964, p.22.
5. Sinha, A.K.,'On the Problem of Cultural Identity with special reference to Ancient Indian and Greek Cultures'. in *Graeco-Indica-Demetrius Galanos Memorial Volume*, (ed.) U.P. Arora, Delhi, 1989. p. 280-81.
6. See, Pande, G.C., *An Approach to Indian Culture and Civilization*, Varanasi, 1985, p.21.
7. Sinha, A.K., *Readings in Early Indian Socio-Cultural History*, Delhi, 2000, p.49.
8. Kangle, R.P., *The Kauṭilya Arthaśāstra*, Part-I, 15.1.1-2.
9. *Ibid.*
10. *Webster's New World Dictionary, Modern Desk Edition.*
11. *Oxford English Dictionary.*
12. *Cambridge Dictionary of Philosophy* (Gen. ed.) Robert Audi.
13. *International Encyclopedia of Social Sciences*, Vol. 16.
14. Gupta, Shantinath, *The Indian Concept of Values*, p.7.
15. Perry, R.B., *Realms of Value*, p.4.
16. Gupta, S.N., *op. cit.*, p.7.
17. *Ibid*, pp.7-8.
18. *Ibid*, p.9.
19. *Ibid.*
20. *Mimansaka Sutra*, 1.1.1-4.
21. Gupta, S. N., *op. cit.*, p.9
22. Maitra, S.K., *The Ethics of the Hindus*, Calcutta, 1963, pp. 81-82
23. *Kāmasūtra*, 2.36.
24. Mahadeva, T.M.P., *Outlines of Hinduism*, pp. 66-67.

25. Perry, R.B., *Realms of Value*, pp. 2-3.
26. Perry R.B., *General Theory of Value*, New York, 1926, p.124.
27. Moore, G.E., *Ethics*, Oxford, 1935, pp. 9-11.
28. He is of view "that universal predicate of value is applicable to these naturalistic objects and definition would takes us into an indefinite regress". Gupta, S.N., *op. cit.*, p.10.
29. Moore, G.E., *Principia Ethica*, London, 1952, pp. 9-10.
30. He is of view that to say something is good or right to say that is commanded by God. - Hartmann, N., *Ethics*, p. 111
31. Gupta, S.N., *op. cit.*, p.11.
32. Sinha, R.P., *The Vedanta of Sankara-A Metaphysics of Value*, vol-I, p. 22.
33. "Essence is the kind of being through which everything participating in it is first as it is".-*Ethics*, Vol-I, pp. 184-185.
34. According to him value emanate neither from the things nor from the percipient...they are not even capable of being directly grasped by thought; rather they are immediately discerned only by inner vision like 'Plato's Ideas'. Therefore value depends on the things that are valuable (good) but are actually their pre-requisites, they are that whereby things...and in the wider sense real entities and relations of every kind...possess the character of 'good', that is they are that through which things are valuable". *Ibid*, pp. 185-186.
35. Gupta, Shanti nath, *op. cit.*, p. 10.
36. Urban, W.M., *Fundamental of Ethics*, New York, 1949, p. 18.
37. Pandey, R.B., *Bhartiya Niti Ka Vikas*, Patna, 1965, p. 4; Nikam, N.A., *Some Concepts of Indian Culture*, Simla, 1973, p. 47.
38. Deveraj, N.K., *Philosophy, Religion and Culture*, Varanasi, 1974, p.1; Mackenzie, *A Manual of Ethics*, London, 1929, p. 218.
39. Pande, G.C., *The Meaning and Process of Culture*, Agra, 1972, p. 2; Nikam, N.A., *op. cit.*, p. 47.
40. Pande, G.C., *op. cit.*, p. 2.
41. Pandey, R.B., *op. cit.*, p. 4; Nikam, N.A., *op. cit.*, p. 47; Pande, G.C., *Mulya Mimamsa*, p. 33.
42. Stace, W.T., *Religion and Modern Mind*, London, 1943, p.26; Devaraj, N.K., *Samskrti Kei Darsanika Vivecana*, Lucknow, 1972, p.48.

43. Mukherjee, Radha, Kamal, *The Social Structure of Values*, Delhi, 1965, pp. 4-5; Durant, Will, *The Pleasure of Philosophy*, Newyork, 1973, pp.76-77; Pandey, R.B., *op. cit.*, p.4.
44. Pande, G.C., *op. cit.*, p.30.
45. cf. Mukherjee, R.K., *op. cit.*, pp. 4-5.
46. "Facts help in the knowledge of value and their whole valuation depends on this fact only".-Hiriyana, M., *op. cit.*, pp. 2-3.
47. Nikam, N.A., *op. cit.*, p. 47.
48. Hiriyana, M., *op. cit.*, p. 47.
49. *Aitereya Āraṇayaka*, 23.2,3; Hiriyana, *op. cit.*, p. 5.
50. Radha Krishanan, S., *An Idealist View of Life*, (reprint) Delhi, 1979, p. 208.
51. Pande, G.C., *op. cit.*, p. 32.
52. Sinha, A.K., *Mulya Kei Avadharna Aur Swaroop*, p. 183.
53. Nikam, N.A., *op. cit.*, p.47; Lillie, William *An Introduction to Ethics*, Delhi, 1975, p.4; Pandey, R.B., *op. cit.*, p.4; Pande, G.C., *op. cit.*, pp. 253-54.
54. Pande, G.C., *op. cit.*, p.75; Radha Krishnan, S., *op. cit.*, p.208.
55. cf., Jain, Sagarmal-Jain, *Bauddha aur Gita Kei Acara-darshna ka Tulnatmak Adhyanana*, (Pt.I) 1982, Jaipur, 1982, p.1.
56. "the subject that gets the support of intellect for being a subject of search is value". -Pande, G.C., *op. cit.*, p.31.
57. Gupta, S. N., *op. cit.*, p.32f.
58. *Taittirīya Upaniṣad*, p.7; Dasgupta, S.N., *A History of Indian Philosophy*, Vol.-1, Delhi, 1975, pp. 46, 60-61.
59. Tylor while discussing religion said that it is a belief in other worldly conscious powers. Describing religion, Sir James Frazer said that it an effort of pleasing those powers about which it is believed that they are higher than man and control man and nature, as quoted by Devaraj, N.K., *Philosophy Religion and Culture*, Varanasi, 1974, pp. 348-49.
60. *Taittirīya Āranayaka*, 2.3.3; Hiriyana, M., *op. cit.*, p. 5; Pande, G.C., *op. cit.*, pp. 30, 63, 75; cf, Radha Krishnan, *op. cit.*, p. 208.
61. *Mahābhārata Śāntiparva*, 294.20; *Hitopadeśa*, 25; Hiriyana, M., *op. cit.*, p.51, Pande, G.C., *Bhartiya Paramparā kei Mula Svara*, Delhi, 1981, p.63.
62. Hiriyana, M., *op. cit.*, p. 5.

63. Mackenzie, J.S., *A Manual of Ethics*, London, 1929, p.170; Sinha, A.K., *Santiparva Mein Visleshit Natik Vicara*, p. 59.
64. Pande, G.C., *Mulya Mimamsa*, p. 55.
65. "Will, independence and conscious effort is the primary condition for the conception of value".Hiriyana, M., *op. cit.*, p.7; Nikam, N.A., *op. cit.*, p.15.
66. Pande, G.C., *The Meaning and Process of Culture*, Agra, 1972, p. 1.
67. Nikam, N.A., *op. cit.*, p. 47.
68. Hiriyana, M., *op. cit.*, p. 5; Nikam, N.A., *op. cit.*, p. 15.
69. Sinha, A.K., Mulya kei Avadharna aur Swaroop, *Journal of Ganga nath Jha Kendriya Sanskrit Vidyapeeth*, Allahabad, 1991, p. 182.
70. RadhaKrishnan, S., *op. cit.*, p.208.
71. Lillie, William, *An Introduction to Ethics*, p. 240.
72. Pande, G.C., *Mulya Mimamsa*, p. 38.
73. "Merely satisfaction of desires is not however, Value, unless the satisfaction is conscious satisfaction". See, Nikam, N.A., *op. cit.*, p.15.
74. Hartmann, *Ethics*, Vol. I, p.220-21; Sabine, G.H., *A History of Political Theory*, New York, 1961, p. 461-63; Pande, G.C., *op. cit.*, p. 64.
75. Barker, E., *Politics of Aristotle*, Oxford, 1946, p. 355 ff.
76. Zimmer, H., *Philosophies of India*, (ed.) J. Campbell (reprint) Newyork, 1976, p. 41; Dandekar, R.N., The Role of man in Hinduism in *Religion of the Hindus* (ed.) K.W. Morgan, New York, 1953, p. 135.
77. Sinha, A.K., *op. cit.*, p. 196.
78. Pandey, R.B., *op. cit.*, p. 55.
79. Devraja, N.K. *Sanskrit Kei Darsanik Vivecana*, Lucknow, 1972 p, 186; Pande, G.C., *op. cit.*, p. 60.
80. See, Hiriyana, M., *op. cit.*, p.249, Maitra, S.K., *The Ethics of the Hindus*, Calcutta, 1963, p.237.
81. cf. Pande, G.C., *op. cit.*, p. 66.
82. Pande, G.C., *op. cit.*, p.249.
83. *Chāndogya Upaniṣad*, p.23.
84. Dandekar, R.N., *op. cit.*, p.135.
85. Hiriyana, M., *op. cit.*, p.1.

86. Hiriyana, M., *op. cit.*, p.2.
87. Sinha, A.K., *op. cit.*, p.187.
88. Majumdar, R.C., *Ancient India*, Delhi, 1962, pp.26-27; Ghosh, N.N., *Early History of India*, Allahabad, 1973, pp.53-54.
89. Sharma, R.S., *Aspects of Political Ideas and Institutions in Ancient India*, Delhi, 1968, p.273; Chakrobarti, Haripada, *Vedic India, Political and Legal Institutions in Vedic Literature*, Calcutta, 1981, p.94.
90. Jayaswal, K.P., *Hindu Polity*, Part II, Banglore, 1943, p.189.
91. *Ṛgveda*, X. 85.36; Hindrey, R., *Comparative Ethics in Hindu and Buddhist Traditions*, Delhi, 1978, p. 48; Kuhanraja, C., *The Vedas*, Waltair, 1957, p.186.
92. Gopal, Lallanji, *Pracina Bhartiya Rajanaitik Vicaradhara*, Delhi, 1999, p.2; Sharma, R.S., *op. cit.*, pp.273-74.
93. Roychowdhry, H.C., *Political History of Ancient India*, pp.75-117.
94. The first reference of the four-fold division has found in the *Purūṣa-sukta* of the *Ṛgveda*. See, *Ṛgveda*, 10.92.12.
95. See, *Aitereya Brāhmaṇa* 35.2; *Taittirīya Saṁhita* 6.2.75, etc.
96. Ghosh, N.N., *op. cit.*, pp.92-96.
97. Majumdar, R.C., *Ancient India*, pp.179-81.
98. See, Roy, U.N., *Gupta Samrata aur unka Kala*, Allahabad., 1986, pp.372-423.

2. The Changing Notions of *Artha*

Artha occupies an important place in the Indian scheme of four-fold values popularly called *Purūṣārtha-Catuṣṭay*. As already stated, in Indian perspective, the conception of value appears before us in the form of the *Purūṣārtha-Catuṣṭay*, which is a wonderful co-ordination of the biological, empirical, and spiritual values[1]. The essential elements of value-consciousness are intellect and freedom of choice[2] and it possesses an inherent relation with human nature[3] and therefore, man, in a natural way, seeks to realize values from the lowest to the highest level corresponding to the development of his nature at the different stages.[4] This may clearly be idealized in the description of the *Pañca-kośa* theory in the *Taittirīya Upaniṣad*[5]. The consciousness of value arising at the different level of these *kośa* may correspondingly be reflected in the system of *Purūṣārtha* propounded by Indian thinkers for the welfare of man. In this scheme of values, viz. *purūṣārtha* along with *dharma* and *kāma*, *artha* is placed in the list of the means supposed necessary to be achieved by man in this world and it is expected from him that after enjoying the pursuits of *trivarga*, he will try to achieve the fourth *varga mokṣa*, a transcendental ideal, listed as the last and final value in *Purūṣārtha-Catuṣṭay*[6].

It is quite true that ancient Indian seers put great emphasis on the spiritual attainment of life and their supreme aim was to transcendent this world of will and desire and attain the ultimate stage of *satcidānanda*[7] but they did not totally discard the achievements of worldly life and held a positive attitude towards worldly life and its problems.[8] They, therefore, acknowledged the importance of material pleasure in life and gave due importance to the values of *artha* and *kāma*.[9] Despite an emphasis on material pleasure it could be realized that its excess will not be beneficial for man having sparks of spiritualism in him. This led to the development of a balanced philosophy of life and caused Indian culture developed in a specific way. Thus, *dharma*[10] was given a higher place and *artha* and *kāma* were brought under its control. In Indian way of life the clear dominance of *dharma* is visible in all aspects and every sphere of life. *Dharma*, in this scheme, is undoubtedly a code of conduct applicable at every age and stage of life but in its primary sense it is inseparably related to the essential and inherent goodness of human nature being the first and foremost quality of his existence. It is *dharma* which differentiates man from the other lower animals otherwise on the primary level of life man has no difference from lower animals other than form and feature.[11] '*Dharma*' here stands for the basic consciousness of man sometimes called *Jñāna*. It is said in the Hitopadesa that, "Hunger, sleep, fear and sex are common to man and beasts.[12] It is *Jñāna* that specially characterizes man and when they lack it, they become one with the beasts". The *Mahābhārata* also speaks the same in the *Śantiparva* where '*Dharma*' is regarded as the highest virtue of man.[13] *Dharma*, therefore, is the human quality enabling man to distinguish between the 'right' and the 'wrong' the 'good' and the 'evil' or the *artha* and the *anartha* in a traditional terminology.[14]

Artha, thus, plays a very important role in Indian philosophy of life and ancient Indian seers realizing the importance of the fulfilment of material desires in life developed a wider connotation of *artha* which included everything desired by man and also the way to fulfil these desires. A high place in Indian way of life was given to the value of *artha* that seems to be generic term meaning 'possession'. Vātsyāyana said, in his *Kāmasūtra*, "*artha* is the acquisition of arts, land, gold, cattle, wealth...and friends. It is also the protection of what is acquired and the increase of what is protected."[15] Therefore, *artha* is desirable for every one. *Artha* has been taken by a group of thinkers mainly spiritualists as an evil that binds man in the world of will and desires and thus creates hindrance in one's way of perfection[16] whereas for another group, i.e. materialists, it is the only real value which is necessary for the survival of man[17] without it the life of man cannot survive.[18] But for both groups '*artha*' is something achievable by man.[19] Thus any achievement whether temporal, empirical or spiritual can be regarded *sārthaka* (meaningful) only when there is a human being to achieve it. If human being is not survived all achievements are meaningless.[20] *Artha* is an important value because it practically makes the survival of life possible. All things, objects, which are supposed necessary for the survival of human being, are included in its fold.

Artha, therefore, is a name for all values belonging to the empirical life. Wealth, power, socio-economic set-up, etc. collectively known as material, biological, political values of life[21] are all included in *artha*. *Artha*, therefore, is a term that has been used for value-in-general in ancient India.

From early Vedic period to the period up to the advent of Islam, India witnessed great changes in the political as well as ideological sphere that played a significant role in bringing significant changes in the notion of *artha* from value-in-general to politico-economic in Kauṭilyan period and finally as wealth in post Kauṭilyan period. In this chapter an attempt will be made to notice these changes in the notion of term *artha* and will also be tried to analyze the 'how and why' of the changes in notion of *artha* that signifies initially value in general and was transformed at later date into a narrow concept of wealth. Keeping this objective in view the aim will be to consider the historical development of the concept of *artha* and emphasis will be given on the changes that have occurred in the ideological and political sphere of the country owing to the historical and cultural development from the beginning to the period under study.

In the initial sense of the word '*artha*' stands for value,[22] because the word '*artha*' is a *Sanskrit* word which stands for 'meaning' and this connotation of *artha* indicates a sense of value. Yāska in his 'Nirukta' used the word '*artha*' for value.[23] In fact in all its usages the word *artha* indicate a sense of value and thus it itself becomes a synonym of value. The necessary predicate of value is 'idea' and 'fact'.[24] *Artha* in itself possesses both these predicates. When it is "used for desire, wish, meaning, reason, etc it is an idea and when it is used as an object, or wealth, or profit, etc., it manifests itself as fact."[25] Therefore, *artha* in itself is both desire and desired,[26] and this is the value of *artha* that makes it a synonym of value. All worldly objects and goods are desired or wished by man; hence they are valuable or attached with *artha*. Objects which are desired by man possessed value hence they may be called *sārthaka* or meaningful, for they have capacity to satisfy human desire. Whatever is desired or desirable is meaningful. Hence *sārthaka* and its opposite is *nirarthaka*, the meaningless or disvalue.[27] Meaningful and meaningless are relative terms which can be understood only with reference to human life because all values are essentially human values.[28] Thus values can be "evaluated only in terms of the needs, wants and demands of human life."[29] Nikam holds that merely the satisfaction of desire is not a value, "unless the satisfaction is conscious satisfaction. Conscious satisfaction is enjoyment." Only man is capable of enjoyment 'therefore' "all values in a significant sense are human values, *Purūṣārtha*."[30] In Indian perspective, whatever is desired by human person for satisfying his needs, wants, demands are included in the notion of *purūṣārtha*, i.e. desired by *purūṣa* or human being. What a human person desired at the most is the *Paramārtha*, the highest *artha* meaning the highest value or ultimate end, the *summum bonum*.[31] Value, also in all its definition, is something which arises "from the satisfaction of wants or desires at every level of human consciousness"[32] and thus *artha* and value can be regarded as synonym. In Indian way of life, all things needed, required or desired by human person come under the broad spectrum of *artha*. Generally *artha* is related to the physical or material aspects of life. In the form of *Paramārtha*, though, it touches the highest spiritual level of human desires but primarily it is used to denote material possessions and is closely related to the material pleasure of life.[33]

Literally, *artha* stands for an object, a thing, a referent, or a substance.[34] In the Amarkośa it is used in the sense of wealth purpose, object or prohibition.[35] Zimmer has pointed out that the term "comprises a whole range of tangible objects that can be possessed, enjoyed and lost, and which we require in daily life, for the upkeeping of a household, raising of a family and discharge of religious duties, all that is necessary for the virtuous fulfilment of lifeṣ obligation."[36] It also signifies that objects through which pleasure can be achieved. The word *artha* thus, "connotes the attainment of riches and worldly prosperity,[37] material advantage, wealth and all that which concern commercial life, business matter, business affair, work, price, etc. and in the sphere of law it means plaint, action, petition,"[38] in the politics it is interest of state. In life, in general, it is utility that is what is useful.[39] With reference to the external world, *artha* in its widest connotation signifies that which can be perceived; an object of senses, with reference to the interior world of psyche, "end and aim, purpose, object, wish, desire, motive, cause, reason, interest, use, want and concern."[40] The term, thus, as pointed out by Zimmer bounds together all the meanings of :

1. The object of pursuit
2. The meaning of this pursuit
3. The needs and the desires suggesting this pursuit.[41]

Potter has suggested that *artha* indicated for Indian "an attitude of minimum concern towards" those things "which are manipulated in making of a living".[42] But this is a very subjective sense in which the term is understood and moreover the term does not so much stand for an attitude as for an end or goal.[43]

Primarily it seems that the term means object in general or sense objects and it is this connotation which continues in the period before Kauṭilya. Kauṭilya in his *Arthaśāstra* defines *artha* technically as the livelihood (*vrittih*) of man and inhabited land.[44] This definition of *artha* restricted its meaning. It, on one hand, relates *artha* with the livelihood of people, it furthers its scope with the inhabited land and at a point the two definitions are merged in one specifically when the term *arthaśāstra*[45] is explained. This turned *artha* a politico-economic value in place of value-in-general.

This meaning of word *artha* continued is post Mauryan period also, although, a sense of wealth too came to be attached with it for land, till then, was being considered as prime source of wealth. The meaning of *artha* and its changing connotation can be understood more elaborately if we keep an eye over the political, economical and social development of the country from the earliest historical period to the period up to the advent of Islam in India.

The earliest period of Indian history[46] is understood to have begun from the age of *Ṛgveda*, which is admittedly the oldest book in the world. According to Aurobindo, "The *Ṛgveda* is the one considerable document that remains to us from the early period of human thought"[47] and is the only source to know the life and culture of the Aryans in that period. *Artha*, in this Veda, is generally used in empirical or material sense. It denotes the wish,[48] goal[49] aim[50], gain,[51] end,[52] wealth,[53] object[54] purpose,[55] limit,[56] etc. In fact all those objects of wealth and prosperity which man wishes to achieve for the fulfilment of his material and empirical needs, either through his labour, earning or barter are *artha*, the pleasure and joy which he gets through the satisfaction of his desires is also included in *artha*[57]. At many places it is used in the sense of object.[58] In various *mantras* it is used to denote work.[59] It is also used in the sense of goal or aim.[60] *Artha* is again used in the general sense of wealth at many places. According to *Ṛgveda*, "wealth (*artha*) is the medium through which sadness can be removed."[61] It is said in the *Ṛgveda* that those who are worthy of wealth do obtain it as wife gets her husband.[62] Further in another *mantra* it is said that those who wished wealth (*artha*) and proceeds towards it fulfil their desires.[63]

Praying to Agni it is desired in the *Ṛgveda* that "one may, through Agni obtain day by day wealth and prosperity attended with glory and abounding in heroes (heroic sons)."[64] *Artha* is also used in the sense of purpose, in various *mantras*, such as, at one place it is said that "the streams flowing heather have gathered together their waters for a common purpose, like the cows that yield all things to man-that yield all things to people."[65]

Thus, in the *Ṛgveda* the word *artha* is used in the various senses and more apparently it can be said that in its fold it includes all that material and worldly possessions that early Aryans desires to achieve and in this way it could be considered the highest value of life to be achieved for getting satisfaction of desires which in turn gave them joy and pleasure. For understanding what the term '*artha*' means for Ṛgvedic Aryans it is quite necessary to have knowledge of the political, social and cultural atmosphere of that age.

The Ṛgvedic Aryans possessed a very positive attitude towards world, worldly life and its problems.[66] They prayed for cows, sons, wealth, happy long life and all other means of worldly pleasures[67] necessary for a life of ease and comfort. They had no interest in other worldly affairs and had even no idea for salvation rather they wished to lead a happy and prosperous material life full of pleasures and joy.[67A] This world's affirmative attitude of the early Aryans was also the need of the day because they were trying to be settling in a new area[68] and for solving the problems of life in an unknown and unwelcome atmosphere it is necessary to possess a world affirmative attitude.[69] For settling here they had fought many wars with the indigenous people who strongly resisted them[70] as is evident from the various hymns of *Ṛgveda*.[71] These Aryans were divided into many *Janas*,[72] the socio-political unit of Ṛgvedic period[73] as reflected from words like *Pañcajanah*, or *janasah*[74] frequently used in the *Ṛgveda*. These Aryans *janas also* fought with one another[75] and thus 'war' and victory in it came to be taken as the most desirable value and also the source of life for them.[76] To achieve victory in these wars was very essential because besides protecting their own existence they brought them material gains,[77] which was an important source of prosperity in those days.

A careful analysis of the text of the *Ṛgveda* reveals the different stages of development of Aryan culture. Some early passages of the *Ṛgveda* depict a society, which was 'semi-nomadic' with a 'non-stratified' social system.[78] People prayed gods for a life full of material pleasures and comfort and *yajñas* which later became most important and highly ritualistic, were very simple.[79] War being a centrally important phenomenon[80] in their lives would have probably played its important role in determining the social status of the warrior and thus warriors would have been occupied highest place in the society.[81] This is quite natural in a society where 'war' was the source of life and one's social position in the society depends on one's association with war and military activities.[82] Thus, in this period war was the central point around which all other activities of society and social life went on. In the early passages of the *Ṛgveda* the different usages of term '*artha*', i.e. in the sense of wish, goal, aim, wealth, etc. make us believe of an empirical or materialistic attitude of early Vedic people who sought all meaningfulness of their lives in achieving wealth or worldly objects. 'War' was the only means to achieve this *artha*[83] and victory in war depended mainly on an organized team that necessitated the development of social-political unit *jana*.[84]

The later stage of Ṛgvedic society reflected through some late passages of *Ṛgveda* depict a settled life based on agriculture as evident from the usages of different terms associated with agriculture.[85] Their social-system was now stratified as evident from the *Purūṣā-Sūkta*[86] that describes the origin of four-fold social system, later known as *Caturvarṇa-Vyavasthā*.

Between these two extreme phases of development, there was a transitional phase which shows how the values and priorities of life of the Aryans were shifted from early nomadic life to a later settled life and their social system got its latest shape in the form of four *varṇas*. The 'battle of ten kings' on the bank of river Paruṣṇi could be taken as the line of demarcation[87] between these two phases as it was only after the victory of king Sudās in this war that the Aryans became able to move towards the mainland from the '*sapt-sandhav*' region and get settled in the conquered area.[88] In this way the process of expansion of Aryans in new area was started as well as accelerated resulting in a re-formation of the mental and social make-up of the Aryans.[89] Thus, an ambition to rule over a vast land was developed in the mind of the Aryans leading to the transformation of tribal state to the territorial.[90]

Changes also occurred in the social structure of Aryans. In the earlier stage society was not divided into various *Varṇas*. Warriors held an important place as they protect '*jana*'. [91] For protecting *jana* they need victory in war and that can be achieved along with their valour with the help of divine favour.[92] This necessity of having divine favour later on gave rise to a group of experts in priestly affairs[93] who through the performance of sacrifices sought the help of divine power for the victory of *Jana*.[94]

After the victory of Sudās in *Dasrājña* war this group of priests, which was although present but was not much prominent, raised to prominence as they were experts in performance of sacrifices[95] resulting in the division of Aryan stock into three groups, *Brahma*, *Kṣtra* and *Viś*[96] which was clearly based on division of labour and this three-fold division, finally, as Purūṣa-Sūkta reveals, gave rise to the four-fold division of the Aryan society originated from a divine being.[97]

This is a very important change as with it an element of divine power was attached with the culture of the Aryans. Now the values of life were shifted from earthly to heavenly level. Still to attain maximum pleasure and joy was the most desirable value[98] but now it came to be idealized in the form of *Svarga*[99] which could be achieved only through the performance of sacrifices. Thus, with the growth of Ṛgvedic society, sacrifices became very prominent and became the only medium through which divine help could be had and this divine favour was essential for everything.[100] Secondly, sacrifices were the only means through which earthly as well as heavenly gains could be achieved. Therefore, priests became important, as they were experts in their performance. But this development was on the social level. Still '*artha*' was used to denote wish, goal, aim, etc. but its idea was some what changed. Initially it was purely material and empirical value now it became a divine-material value, as the culmination of life was *svarga*, a place full of joy, pleasure and comfort, i.e. all those things that people desired (*artha*). The notion of *artha*, which initially was empirical concept, now transformed into a divine-material and empirical notion.[101] This concept of *Svarga*, which came forward in the co-ordinate form of worldly heavenly pleasures, mingled the idea of other-worldly element in the concept of *artha*. Now the priorities of the life of the Aryans were shifted from worldly to heavenly plane.[102] Hence a sense of divine element was got included in the notion of *artha*. This is an important change, which indicates that the culture and society of the Aryans were developing. A change in the priorities of life clearly reflects a change in the socio-political atmosphere of period that equally made changes in the mentality of the people. This change of values also indicated that the life of the Aryans got settled and they were getting sufficient time to ponder over the matters other than war. It also pointed out a decrease in the frequency of wars and Aryan's hold as well as proper and peaceful administration over the conquered area as without a peaceful atmosphere these types of changes couldn't be prevailed.

The decrease in frequent wars led to the development of an agriculture-based society which was the backbone of the later Vedic age.[103] In the later Vedic age many changes came in the life of the Aryans. On political level an important change was the transformation of tribal-rural polity of Ṛgvedic days into the territorial states of later Vedic period.[104] The '*Jana*' *rajyas* of Ṛgvedic period developed as 'Janapadas' and some big *Janapadas*[105] like Kāṣi, Kośala, Kurū, Pañcala, etc. came in existence. Secondly, in place of war and military activities, agriculture and related activities became more important.[106] The tribal character of polity was replaced by a monarchical system and there was a gradual growth in king's power; and administrative and revenue systems were evolved.[107] King no longer remained merely a military chief rather he became the head of civil and judicial administration. Words like *Virāta*, *Rajñi*, *Sāmrāṭa*, *Sarva rājña*, *Adhipati*[108] etc. reflect the development of political power. Titles like *Adhirāja*,[109] *Ekrāṭ*[110] (sole emperor) *Samrāṭa*[111] (emperor) *Sarvarāja*,[112] *Prajāpati*[113] (Lord of Subjects) frequently referred to in later Vedic texts show that there was tremendous growth in political power. References of growth of different *Yajñas* like *Rājasūya*,[114] *Vājpeya*,[115] *Aśwamedha*[116] *Purūsamedha*, *Sarvamedha*[117] etc. which were performed by the king for proclaiming his sovereignty as well as for the maintenance of his territory are frequently found in the later Vedic texts. Thus, a sacrificial culture was developed in which for achieving anything in life one needed to perform sacrifices which till now had become very complex and highly ritualistic affair to be performed by the experts only and thus, brāhmaṇas, as the experts became most prominent class of the society.[118]

Still *artha* was the most desirable thing and its connotations such as wish, aim, goal, end, purpose, wealth, etc. continued in this age also. The meaningfulness of *artha* as worldly achievements which was the highest objective of early people was also visible in later *Saṁhitas* and *Brāhmaṇ* texts where the word '*artha*' is used for wealth and other desired articles.[119] In the early phase of later Vedic period no significant change occur in the material life as well as mentality of people and their world-affirmative attitude towards life and its problem remained continue. The other worldly element in the life of the Aryans gave rise to the notion of *svarga* which as a culmination of material pleasure, prevailed in this phase also. Concepts of *svarga* and 'godhood' were popular among the masses and were regarded as the highest objective to be achieved in the life[120] and people directed their efforts towards their achievement.

These objectives could be achieved only through the performance of sacrifices. Thus, sacrifice and its rituals became more and more elaborated. The performance of these sacrifices became expensive, difficult as well as time consuming, as there were many references of sacrifices that continued for two or more years. With these elaborate rituals and complexities, *Yajñas* transformed into a mechanical process in which the status of God (for receiving whose blessing these *Yajñas* were performed) became secondary and the performance of rituals became primary. So the respect, faith and tribute for Gods, whose manifestation was the principal objective, found no place in this thinking. In this way *Yajñas*, which were the medium for achieving the divine favour became an important source of the livelihood of priests and social prestige of the performer. As they became very expensive, thus, a person having sufficient wealth could only perform them. They were beyond the limits of a common man. This paved the way for the development of a symbolic form of sacrifices[121] and in the later parts of some important *Brāhmaṇ* texts we find a tendency of higher thought which passing through the *Āraṇayakas* attained its culmination in the *Upaniṣads.*[122]

In the beginning of the later Vedic period, no doubt, some changes occurred in the life and culture of the Aryans but no significant change could appear in the general mentality of people and concepts of *svarga* and godhood remained popular among the masses. *Artha* in this phase was same divine-material-empirical notion as it was in Ṛgvedic period because still material achievements were considered to be the most important. A significant change occurred in the notion of *artha* in the later phase of later Vedic period, i.e. in the period of *Āraṇayakas* and *Upaniṣads*. In this period there was a shift in the values of life of the Aryans. A thoughtful movement started against *Yajñas* and their ritualistic performance. With the development of notions like *Antrayajña* and *manoyajña*, *yajñas*[123] came to be established as a symbolic entity and from material plane they were shifted to mental plane. *Aitereya Āraṇayaka* while declaring *yajña* as the centre of the world connects it with the process of the creation of the world. As human being was a result of this creation, *yajña* and human person was related to each other. This idea gave rise to the view that the power of God, which was tried to be evoked through *yajña*, was a manifestation of the supreme and the sole power that created this world and also reside inside the inner consciousness of human being. So in place of performing outward rituals one should try to evoke one's inner consciousness. This made *Yajñas* only as a symbolic entity.

This transformation that was started in this phase culminated in the philosophy of *Upaniṣads* where knowledge replaced outer rituals of sacrifices. According to Upaniṣads the supreme soul (*Ātman*) of being is the expression of this highest power and the union of Brahman-Ātman is *mokṣa* which is the most desirable, rather ultimate achievement. Thus, an idea of *Paramārtha*, *Param* the highest and *artha* the attainment, developed with a qualitative change in the nature of desirable. i.e. *artha*. This marked a qualitative difference between *artha* and *Paramārtha* by confining the former to the objects of will and desire and the latter to the transcendental attainments as the *summum bonum* of life. It is transcendental because it is a spiritual uplift and regeneration of human being which can only be attained by negating this worldly life, its joy and sorrow.[124] With this shift in the mental make-up of the people, the notion of *artha* also changed. For those who want to achieve material gains only the notion of *artha* was same but for those who want to attain spiritual goals *artha* transformed in the notion of '*Paramārtha*' i.e. the highest spiritual objective. The notion of *artha* thus, was also uplifted and shifted above to the higher level of spiritual achievement.

The meaningfulness of *artha* increased with this and it achieved the highest meaning in the form of *Paramārtha*. This gave rise to the hierarchy of values where the path of good was sharply contrasted with that of pleasures derived from the worldly achievements. This distinction is clearly visible in the *Kathopaniṣad*[125] which established the superiority of *śreyas* over *preyas*. The concept of good (*śreya*) implies something beyond the pleasurable and painful and can be found only in the essence of self (*Ātman*). The path of *śreyas* was, therefore, the path of self-realization and self knowledge[126] while the path of satisfaction (*preyas*) led to the fulfilment of desires relating to worldly ends and transitory pleasures[127] only so it did not lead to the self-realization of one's own self. Śreyas is, thus, more valuable then *preyas*. If an effort is made to understand the meaning of *śreyas* and *preyas* according to Upaniṣadic terminology then *preyas* could be equated with the *artha*, i.e. worldly achievements or common good and *śreyas* could be equated with the *Paramārtha* or the highest good.[128]

Undoubtedly, Upaniṣads had developed a philosophy which put emphasis on spiritual achievements[129] of life but it did not totally discard the worldly achievements or held a world-negating philosophy[130] as misconceptionally understood by some scholars. Rather, it inspired man to achieve a higher level of consciousness through his upliftment from mere worldly desires i.e., advancement from *artha* to *Paramārtha*.[131] Still *artha* in the form of common good was popular among masses and was used in a variety of senses in different *Upaniṣads*. In the *Bṛhadāraṇyaka Upaniṣad*[132] and *Chāndogya Upaniṣad*[133] *artha* is used for purpose. In the *Maitarāyaṇi Upaniṣad*, it is used for object of senses.[134] In *Kathopaniṣad* it is taken to mean material value or empirical gain.[135] In the *Iśa Upaniṣad*[136] it appeared in its previous notion, i.e. object in general. In the same *Upaniṣad* it is also used for matter. In the *Praśana*

Upaniṣad[137] *artha* is used for object. In *Muṇḍaka Upaniṣad* it is used for goal, aim[138] and for highest soul.[139] In the *Śvetāśvatara Upaniṣad* it is used for object,[140] aim,[141] hidden knowledge[142] (mysterious knowledge). This clearly depicts that notion of *artha* as common good was still prevalent and in various *Upaniṣads* it had been existed in its multi-dimensional form. So it is quite clear that in the period of *Upaniṣads artha* was used in a wider perspective and its scope further increased with the mingling of spiritual and transcendental element which gave rise to the notion of *Paramārtha* and in the form of it *artha* touches the highest level, of human desires.

It is true that Upanisadic philosophy reveals a gradation of values in material and spiritual values. But this gradation could be fully revealed in the concept of *Purūṣārtha-Catuṣṭay* at a later date when a synthesis between the empirical and spiritual attainment could take place and a result to it a developed value-system could emerge in a systematic form. In this system of *Purūṣārtha* the basic idea of *artha* as an 'end' was replaced by the idea of 'means'.[143] *Artha* due to the development of another idea of *kāma*[144] as the highest physical level of satisfaction to be achieved by a man became only a 'means', to it, helping in the achievement of *Kāma.*[145] This brought a change in the form of *artha* which now appeared as an instrumental rather than an intrinsic value of early days.[146] This change in the meaning of *artha* was very significant as it continued in the later age and it was only through this change that *artha* lost its independent status of 'value in general' and became only a part of *Purūṣārtha Catuṣṭay* which was a combination of different values and wherein *artha* remained to be one of the four values, essential for material well-being of human being. It makes an individual equipped to attain his satisfaction, joy and pleasure of life viz. *Kāma* that includes in its fold all the things related to the fulfilment of all human wants[147] and needs and achieving satisfaction of this urge was considered as the ultimate desire of an individual.

In the Epics, *artha* was used in the general sense of wealth. In the Rāmāyaṇa it is said that all actions proceed from *artha* (wealth) as rivers emanate from the mountains.[148] All actions of the persons of dull interest not possessent of *artha* (wealth) become unsuccessful as the small rivulets dry up in the summer season.[149] A person who holds wealth has a number of friends and relations to cherish him. A person who possesses adequate wealth is superior person in the world[150], further it is said that a person who has a collection of wealth is considered to be powerful, wise, fortunate and a most talented person.[151] Similar views are expressed in the *Mahābhārata*.[152] In the *Śāntiparva* of the *Mahābhārata* while describing the importance of *artha* (wealth) Arjun said that *artha* was the only medium through which a person could achieve *dharma*, *kāma* and *svarga*. It is impossible to live life without wealth.[153] There are many references in the *Mahābhārata* which clearly established the necessity and importance of *artha* (wealth) in one's life.[154] There is no doubt that the *Mahābhārata* emphasizes the necessity of wealth in one's life and says that all works could be done only with the help of wealth but to regulate it, the *Mahābhārata* puts *artha* under the hold of *Danda*.[155] Though in *Mahābhārata* '*artha*' was used mostly in the sense of wealth or material gain but it was also used in different usages like goal,[156] reference,[157] *Purūṣārtha*,[158] object,[159] meaningful,[160] purpose[161] at many places. Thus in the *Mahābhārata*, *artha* has been regarded as a value which is an instrument to individual and social prosperity and material happiness so it can be termed as an instrumental value.[162] In life, wealth (*vitta*) helps one is attaining other values like charity, hospitality, sacrifice, happiness, kindness, satisfaction of desires, etc. Therefore, the *Mahābhārata* recommends *artha* as a normal object of human pursuit but simultaneously it warns that it (wealth) should not be treated as an intrinsic value. It should be pursued only as instrument to realize *dharma* and *kāma*.[163]

So in the period of Epics, *artha* was used in various senses although the most prominent sense was in the form of wealth that transformed *artha* into a value essential for livelihood of man for his survival. Another important change that occurs in this period was the mingling of political thinking in the notion of *artha* and this caused further change in the notion of *artha* in which *artha* became a politico-economic value. The chapter 59 of the *Śāntiparva* of the *Mahābhārata* refers *arthaśāstra* as *rājyaśāstra*[164] and present a mythological origin of *arthaśāstra* that will be discussed later on. Thus, a thinking developed later on in which *artha* came to mean a notion relating peripherally to the area of political thought that attained its maturity in the *Arthaśāstra* of Kauṭilya which significantly used the word *artha* to mean a politico-economic value. *Arthaśāstra* in this sense appeared as the science of polity. It is in this sense that the *Rāmāyana* used the word *Arthaśāstra*. It mentions Sudhanva, the teacher of Rāma well versed in the *arthaśāstra*.[165] This clearly shows that it was treated as a branch of learning at that time. Besides that at many places, '*artha*' was used for money, cattle, etc.[166]

It is quite true that elements of political speculation was already present in the idea of word *artha* prior to the period of Kauṭilya. The *Mahābhārata* clearly describes the origin of *arthaśāstra* in the form of rājyaśāstra[167] and it was not a sudden development. As will be discussed later, there was a complete tradition behind it.[168] But it is also true that it was only the *Arthaśāstra* of Kauṭilya that gave this tradition a sound basis as well as a systematic form.[169] Kauṭilya himself declares his *Arthaśāstra* as a compendium written after compiling almost all the works of his predecessors.[170] It was the first available treatise belonging to the polity and statecraft and was a practical handbook rather than a theoretical testimony.[171] In his treatise Kauṭilya has used the word '*artha*' in a very technical sense.[172] According to him *artha* is *manuṣyānāma vṛtti* and *manuṣyavati bhumi*, i.e. livelihood or sustenance of man and inhabited land both is *artha*.[173] Kauṭilyan idea of *artha* can be better understood only in the framework of the political and cultural situations of the age. There is a great controversy among the scholars regarding the date of Kauṭilya's *Arthaśāstra* that will be discussed later on.[174] But without involving in that it may safely be assumed that the major portion of the treatise was composed during the Mauryan age when India had witnessed political unity under the rule of powerful Mauryan kings.[175] As tradition spoke, Kauṭilya was the teacher as well as the prime minister of Candragupta Maurya, the founder of the Mauryan dynasty, therefore, the problem before Kauṭilya was to manage state affairs and protect this newly founded kingdom so he wrote a practical testimony[176] to guide emperor in every situation.[177] Up to the age of Kauṭilya king had been considered responsible for everything, beneficial or unbeneficial, that occurred in his kingdom.[178] The prime responsibility of a king was to maintain law and order in the society so that their remained peace, harmony, and people could earn their riches easily.[179] The Kauṭilyan concept of *artha* can be understood only by relating it to the state and politics. This notion of *artha* includes in itself both manpower and inhabited land or earthly resources. Both were essential for state for these two elements constitute the backbone of state economy.[180] As Kauṭilya was realist in approach, he was well aware of the importance of both these resources in the development of a country.[181] This unparallel importance of these resources was already realized in the later Vedic period when the tribal states were transformed into territorial[182] and geographical element was included in them as evident from word *rastra*[183] which meant a particular state had a certain geographical location.[184] This also indicated that the people of those states had developed skill in agricultural activities for which they needed more and more land for cultivation. Hence an agriculture-based society was being emerged slowly. With an increase in the importance of land[185] as the main source of prosperity imperialist tendencies grew that resulted in the development of sixteen Mahājanapadas in the age of Buddha. The stages of the rise of Magadha as sole power among these *janapadas* and finally in the unification of country under the rule of imperial Mauryas are well known to the students of Indian history. According to Kauṭilya livelihood of man is '*artha*' because without it survival of life is not possible. It is *vritti* through which men earned their riches.[186] It is said in *Cāṇakyasutra* that the root of *artha*-benefits is *Vṛtti.*[187] It is related intimately with *Vārta*[188] which as a totality of the agriculture, cattle-rearing and trade and commerce, is highly important for state for the development of a sound economic-system to fulfil the basic requirements of its subjects and also for developing into a prosperous state.

It is *manuṣyavati bhumi* or inhabited land that provided financial as well as physical support for the sound footing and proper development of state, therefore, it is worthy to be called *artha.*[189] In fact according to Kauṭilya's definition of *artha*, the earth, giver of wealth, grains, clothes, house, property, etc. is real '*artha*'.[190] Kauṭilya regarded land as most important among all other things because land is the only permanent entity and all the other means of livelihood of men grow from it only. So in the view of Kauṭilya land is primary object and all the other things are secondary.[191] This importance of land is also testified in the organic concept of state in which *janapada* has been included among the seven constituents of state.[192] Due to this importance of *manuṣyānāma vṛtti* and *manuṣyavati bhumi* Kauṭilya regarded them as *artha* and in his treatise he described the measures of protecting and maintaining this '*artha*'. So he named his treatise as *Arthaśāstra* and gave a distinct meaning to the word '*artha*' to denote a sense of politico-economic value.

After the decline of Mauryan Empire, a tendency of decentralization appeared in India. In the absence of any strong centralized political power a period of political disunity and confusion prevailed inviting foreigners to invade the country. As a result India witnessed many foreign invasions that of Kuṣāṇas, Indo-Greeks, Sakas, etc.[193] Later on these foreigners settled down in the country and adopted Indian culture and way of life. Small kingdoms also arose in various areas. On social level we find slight changes in the *Varṇa* system resulting into the assimilation of non-Vedic people (foreign *yavanas* and Indigenous tribes) in its fold. In the period of Brahaminical revival,[194] as shown by different texts of this period,[195] *Varṇa-dharma* was attached with *manuṣyānāma vṛtti* and in place of *rājadharma, Varṇa-dharma* became primary and its performance was also considered to be a personal affair,[196] which, according to Kauṭilya,[197] was a duty of state in earlier days. Due to lack of any centralized political power individuality prevailed and dominated every sphere of life.[198] This individualism gave rise to the principal of individual ownership of land. Thus, a class of landlords was created[199] that paved the way for the rise of feudalism in the later centuries.[200] These changes caused a significant change in the Kauṭilyan concept of *artha* as *manuṣayānāma vṛtti* and *manuṣyavati bhumi*, its scope was further narrowed, and it was now taken most prominently to mean wealth.[201]

It is for this reason only that in the post-Kauṭiliyan age, *artha* was prominently used to mean wealth although other meanings are also not completely out of use. Amarkośa[202] used *artha* as a synonym of wealth, object, purpose and prohibition. Kāmandaka in his *Nitisāra* took *artha* as a synonym of wealth or kośa.[203] He also advised the king to always protect his kośa for religious ceremonies, increasing of wealth (*artha*) and for looking after his subjects.[204] Somadeva also regarded *artha* as a thing essential for fulfilling the entire human needs and desires.

According to Śukra, *arthaśāstra* was the science which teaches along with kingly duties, how to earn money.[205] In the view of Śukra, man should possess wealth along with virtues because everyone discards poor person.[206] Therefore, for worldly life wealth is very important and man should try to earn wealth (*artha*) through all truthful means.[207] *Bṛhaspati sūtra* also said that a wealthy person have friends, *dharma*, knowledge, virtues. A person who does not possess wealth is equal to a dead person or a *candāla*. So wealth or *artha* is the root of the world.[208] Manu also accepted the importance of wealth (*artha*) in one's life.[209] *Kāmasūtra* said that *artha* is the acquisition of arts, land, gold, cattle, grains, household articles and friends.[210] In his *Meghaduta* and *Raghuvaṃsa*, Kālidāsa also used *artha* in the sense of wealth.[211] While telling about the importance of *artha* he described different measures that a king could use for acquiring finance and fulfilling his kośa. The king, according to him, could take one sixth of the agriculture, could put taxes on bridges, commerce, etc.[212]

Bhāravi in his *Kirātarjuniyam* also emphasized the importance of wealth and power. According to him "the man who wishes to effort his rise (to wealth and power) should first dispel the darkness of anger by (the light of) his intellect. He who although powerful, does not resist the encroachment of the darkness of delusion arising from anger destroys all the wealth and power as the dark half (of a month) does all the digits of moon."[213]

A verse attributed to Vyās by the editor of *Subhāsitāratnabhāndagāra* recommends "the wiseman should pursue knowledge and wealth with the perseverance worthy of an immortal."[214] Bharthari have aptly said in his *Nitiśatakam* that a person who has wealth is noble.[215] A wealthy person have all virtues in him thus all virtues are related to wealth.[216] So in post Kauṭiliyan age *artha* was mostly used in the sense of wealth and this meaning of *artha* continued in later centuries.

This account of the notion of *artha* and its changing connotations evidently show how this wider notion which originally and initially used for 'value in general' transformed into material empirical value then into divine-material-empirical, then enhanced to spiritual level but afterwards it came to appear in a much narrow concept of politico-economic value and finally in the notion to mean wealth. Although it remained to be a 'value' in all its connotations but its scope never remained the same. Political, economic, social and cultural conditions of the country played its role in changing the connotations of word *artha*. In fact the real significance of '*artha*' can be understood only by keeping these conditions in mind. As every connotation of word reflected the socio-political conditions of the time hence without having a reference to these, it is not possible to grasp the changes in the meaning of the word *artha* for all meaningfulness of a value invariably depends on the situations from which it emerges and these changes in the notions of *artha*, caused changes in the notions of *arthaśāstra* too.

NOTES AND REFERENCES

1. Gupta, Shantinath, *The Indian Concept of Values*, Delhi, 1978, p.1.
2. Pande, G.C., *Mulya Mimamsa*, Jaipur, 1973, p.31.
3. Pandey, Rajbali, *Bhartiya Niti Ka Vikas*, Patna, 1965, p.4.
4. Pande, G.C., *op. cit.*, p.22; Sinha, A.K., Mulya Kei Avadharna

aur Swaroop, in the *Journal of Ganganath Jha Kendriya Sanskrit Vidyapeetha*, Allahabad, p.182.

5. *Taittiriya Upaniṣad*, 2-7; Dasgupta, S.N., *A History of Indian Philosophy*, Vol.-1, Delhi, 1975, p.46.
6. Gupta, S.N., *op. cit.*, P.1; Hiriyana, M., *Indian Conception of Values*, Mysore, 1975, p.266; Ayer, P.S.S., *Evolution of Hindu Moral Ideals*, p.153.
7. Radhakrishnan, S., *An Idealist View of Life*, p.3; cf., Deveraja, N.K., *Sanskriti Kei Darsanik Vivecana*, Lucknow, 1972, p.186.
8. Various passages of *Vedic* literature clearly show that Aryans held a positive attitude towards life and they demanded pursuits of material life from gods. Moreover, in the Upaniṣads also, that are regarded as *mokṣaśāstras* it is expected that one would try to attain '*Brahman*' only after fulfilling his worldly duties and obligations.
9. Gupta, S.N., *op. cit.*, p.2-3; Verma, Jaya, *Pracina, Bharat mein Mulya Cetna aur Artha*, New Delhi, 2001, p.135.
10. '*Dharma*' for Indian is not merely a religion or religious sect. It possesses a wider significance and signifies moral duty, obligation, etc., for various meanings of '*Dharma*' see, Kane, P.V., *History of Dharmasastra.*, Vol.-I, Pt-I, pp. 1-4.
11. *Aitereya Āraṇayaka*, 2.3.2; Hiriyana, M., *Indian Conception of Values*, p.5.; Pande, G.C., *Bhartiya Parampara Kei Mula Svara*, p.63.
12. *Hitopadeśa*, 25; Hiriyana, M., *op. cit.*, p.5.
13. *Mahābhārata, Śāntiparva*, 294.20.
14. Maitra, S.K., *The Ethics of the Hindus*, Calcutta, 1963, p.88.
15. Vātsyāyana's *Kāmasūtra* 1.1.
16. Gupta, S.N., *op. cit.*, p.58.; Sinha, A.K., *Readings in Early Indian Socio-Cultural History*, New Delhi, 2000, p.47.
17. Deveraja, N.K., *Philosophy, Religion & Culture*, Varanasi, 1974, p.1.
18. Gupta, S.N., *op. cit.*, pp.58-59.
19. Sinha, A.K., *op. cit.*, p.47.
20. Sinha, A.K., *op. cit.*, pp.48-49.
21. Gupta, S.N., *op. cit.*, p.62.
22. Pande, G.C., *Mulya Mimamsa*, p.5.; Sinha, A. K., *op. cit.* p. 48.
23. Pande, G.C., *op. cit.*, p.5.; also quoted in his *Bhartiya*

Parampara Kei Mula Svara, p.60.

24. Schiller, F.C.S., 'Value' *in Encyclopedia of Religion and Ethics,* Vol. 12, p.584; Gupta, S.N., *op. cit.,* p.18.
25. Sinha, A.K., *op. cit.* pp.48-49.
26. Maitra, S.K., *op. cit.,* pp.87-88.; Gupta, S.N., *op. cit.,* p.9.
27. Sinha, A.K., *op. cit.,* p.49.
28. Nikam, N.A., *Some Concepts of Indian Culture,* Simla, 1973, p.47.
29. Hiriyana, M., *op. cit.,* p.2; Sinha, A.K. *op. cit.,* p.49. Pandey, R.B., *op. cit.,* p.4; Mukherjee, R.K., *The Social Structure of Values,* p.4-5; Durrant, Will, *The Pleasures of Philosophy,* New York., 1973, pp.76-77.
30. Nikam, N.A., *op. cit.,* p.47.
31. Sinha, A.K., *op. cit.,* p.47.
33. Gopal, Lallanji, and Yadav, B.N.S., *Bhartiya Sanskrti,* Gorakhpur, 1962, p.27.
34. Sinha, A.K., *op. cit.,* p.48.
35. *Amar Kośa,* 3.3.86.
36. Zimmer, H., *Philosophies of India,* (ed.) Campbell, J., Network, 1953, p.35.
37. Gupta, S.N., *op. cit.,* p.48.
38. Pant A.D., *A Critical Study of Arthaśāstra Tradition in Ancient Indian Political Thought,* (Unpublished D.Litt. Thesis) Allahabad, 1966, pp.139-140.
39. Gokhale, B.G., *Indian Through Ages,* pp.54-55.
40. Pant, A.D., *op. cit.,* p.140; Gupta, S.N., *op. cit.,* p.48.
41. Zimmer, H., *op. cit.,* pp.35-36.
42. Potter, K.H., *Presuppositions of India's Philosophies,* New Delhi, 1965, as quoted by Pant, A.D., *op. cit.,* p.140.
43. Pant, A.D., *op. cit.,* p.140.
44. *The Kautiliya Arthaśāstra,* 15.1, (ed.) Kangle, R.P., Pt-I.
45. *The Kautiliya Arthaśāstra,* 15.1.
46. Harappan period is not included in this study as its script is yet not deciphered satisfactorily and without any literary evidence, it is quite difficult to say anything with certainty about their culture.
47. Sri Aurobindo, On the *Veda,*
48. *Ṛgveda,* 1.102; 105.2.

49. *Ṛgveda*, 1.38.2; 2. 30.2; 3.53.5; 6.1.3; 6.32.5; 7.18.9, 63.4; 10.51. 4,73.5, 143.1.
50. *Ṛgveda*, 1.158.6; 7.63.4.
51. *Ṛgveda*, 1.113.6
52. *Ṛgveda*, 1.130.5, 158.6
53. *Ṛgveda*, 3.11.3; 8.69.17.
54. *Ṛgveda*, 4.13.3, 10.27.20.
55. *Ṛgveda*, 1.124.1; 2.39.1.
56. *Ṛgveda*, 10.184.
57. *Ṛgveda*, 5.53.5.
58. *Ṛgveda*, 2.39.1.
59. *Ṛgveda*, 9.1.5.; 10.91.5, 4.13.3.
60. *Ṛgveda*, 3.52.5; 10.22.6.
61. *Ṛgveda*, 3.11.3.
62. *Ṛgveda*, 1.105.2.
63. *Ṛgveda*, 8.79.5.
64. *Ṛgveda*, 1.1.3.
65. *Ṛgveda*, 1.30.5, also in 1.124.1, 2.39.1 .
66. Raju P.T., 'The Concept of Man in Indian Thought' in *The Concept of Man* (ed.) RadhaKrishnan, S., and Raju, P.T., London, 1966, p.233.; Kunhanraja, C., *The Vedas, Waltair,* 1957, p.186.; Pandey, R.B., *op. cit.*, p.41.
67. *Ṛgveda*, 1.79.4, 98.1, 92.13, 157.2; 3.1.19; 4.8.7; 5.10.1, 23.2; 6.10.5, 16.20; 7.41.3, 72.1; 8.5.10, 15;9.4.3, 13.5.
67A. Pande, G.C., *op. cit.*, p.30; Aiyer, P.S.S., *op. cit.*, p.166; Keith, A.B., *The Religion and Philosophy of the Veda and Upanisads,* p. 480.
68. There is a strong controversy regarding the original home of Aryans. A.C. Das, G.N. Jha, etc., support indigenous origin theory while other group of scholars hold that they came in India from outside but which was the original home of Aryans is also a matter of great controversy. See Majumdar, R.C., (ed.) *The Vedic Age*, Chapter 10; *Chakraborti*, H., *Vedic India-Political and Legal Institutions in Vedic Literature*, Calcutta, 1981, Chapter, 1, pp.1-20.
69. Sinha, A.K., *op. cit.*, p.17.

    There are many passages in *Ṛgveda*, which reflect that Aryans fought many wars with non-Aryans for settling here, see,

Ṛgveda. 4.16. 13., 4.30. 21, etc.

70. Chakraborti, H.P., *op. cit.*, p.28.
71. *Ṛgveda*, 1.43, 130.7; 2.14.6, 19.6; 4.16.13; 30.21.
72. Reference to '*Jana*' is found in many hymns such as 3.43.5, 19.; 9.35.5, etc.
73. Chakraborti, H.P., *op. cit.*, p.94; also Sharma, R.S., *Aspects of Political Ideas and Institutions in Ancient India*, p.264.
74. Majumdar, R.C., (ed) *The Vedic Age*, p.359; Ghurye, G.S., *Vedic India*, Bombay, 1979, pp.181-189; Chakraborti, *op. cit.*, p.94; Bhargava, P.L., *India in the Vedic Age*, pp.294-295.
75. Chakraborti, H.P., *op. cit.*, p.57; Sharma, R.S., *op. cit.*, pp.264-265.
76. Sinha, A.K., *op. cit.*, p.17.
77. *Ṛgveda*, 10.101.17; Atharva *Veda*, 20.11.9-11; Roy, B.P., *Later Vedic Economy*, Patna, 1984, p.84.
78. Sharma, R.S., *op. cit.*, p.264; Romila Thapar prefers to name it as 'lineage society' on certain grounds. See, Thapar, Romila, *From Lineage to State*, Dehli, 1984, p.18.
79. Ghurye, G.S., *op. cit.*. pp.180-189.
80. Sinha, A.K., *op. cit.*, p.20.
81. Gokhale, B.G., Ancient India–History and Culture, (Reprint), Bombay, 1970, p.24; Hopkins, E.W., *The Social and Military Positions of the Ruling Castes in Ancient India*, Varanasi, 1972 pp.125f.
82. Sharma, R.S., *op. cit.*, p.271; Durant, Will, *Our Oriental Heritage*, New York, 1954, pp.21.23.
83. Sinha, A.K., *op. cit.*, p.20.
84. Sharma, R.S., *op. cit.*, p.262.
85. *Ṛgveda*, 3.2. 15., 10.34.13., 101.3; see also, Majumdar G.P., 'Origin and Development of Agriculture in Ancient India' in *Proceedings of All India Oriental Conference*, 1951, pt. III, pp.133-116.
86. *Ṛgveda*, X.90.12.
87. Sinha, A.K., *op. cit.*, p.17.
88. Sharma, V.C., *The Dasarajña War*, Aligarh, 1985, p.28; also, Ragozin, Z.A., *Vedic India*, Delhi, 1961, p.332.
89. Roy, B.P., *Later Vedic Economy*, p.7.
90. *Ṛgveda*, 10.173.1-2, word '*Rastra*' is used which suggests that

territorial idea appears at the end of the period as shown by Sharma, R.S., *op. cit.* p.266; Roy, B.P., *op. cit.*, p.7; Rao, V.B., *Uttar Vedic Samaja evam Sanskriti: Ek Adhyayana*, Varanasi, 1966, p.163.

91. Anand, S., *Ksatriyas in Ancient India*, Delhi, 1985, p.11.
92. *Ṛgveda*, 3.53.18; also Pavgee, N.B., *Self government in Indiå Vedic and Post Vedic*, (reprint), Delhi 1980 p.57, as quoted by Sinha, A.K., *op cit.* p.30, fn. 63.
93. Clayton, A.C., *op. cit.*, p.106; Deshmukh, P.R., *Indus Civilization, Ṛgveda and the Hindu Culture*, Nagpur, 1982, p. 377.
94. Kosambi, D.D., *An Introduction to Indian History*, (2nd ed.), Bombay, 1975, p.24; Sinha, A.K., Dharma, Rajdharma and process of State formation in Ancient India, *Bharti* Vol. 1, Varanasi, 1983, p.52; Clayton, A.C., *The Ṛgveda and the Vedic Religion* Delhi, 1984, p.14.
95. Chakraborti, H. *op. cit.*, p.50; Clayton, A.C., *op. cit.*, p.14;
96. It seems that initially there were only two groups, *Brahma* and *Ksatra* that have been mentioned in the Bṛhaspati Hymn of the *Ṛgveda. see, Ṛgveda*, 4.50.8; Basu, J., *India in the Age of the Brahmanas*, Delhi, p.9;
97. Sinha, A.K., *op. cit.*, p.19.
98. *op. cit.* p.20.
99. Kunhanraja, C., *op. cit.*, p.29; Drekmeier, C., *Kingship and Community in Early India*, p.13.
100. Basham, A.L., *The Wonder that was India*, p.241.
101. Verma, Jaya, *Pracina Bharat mein Mulya Cetna aur Artha*, p.141.
102. Sinha, A.K., *op. cit.*, pp.19-20.
103. Roy, B.P., *Later Vedic economy*, p.84 ff
104. Sharma, R.S., *op. cit.*. p.272.
105. Gopal, Lallaji, *Pracina Bhartiya Rajanatik Vicaradhara*, Varanasi, 1999, p.3.
106. Majumdar, G.P., 'Origin and Development of agriculture in Ancient India' in *Proceedings of All India Oriental Conference*, 1951, Pt III pp 113-116; Ganguli, R., 'Cultivation in Ancient India' in Indian *Historical Quarterly*, Vol. VI, (Reprint), Delhi, 1985 p.137.

107. Pant, A.D., *A Critical Study of Arthaśāstra Tradition in Ancient Indian Political Thought* (unpublished. D. Litt thesis) Allahabad, 1966, p.17.
108. *Yajur veda*, 14.13, 8.37, etc.
109. *Ṛgveda*, 10.128.9; Atharva*veda*, 6.98.1, 9.10.84.
110. *Ṛgveda*, 8.37.3; *Artharvaveda*, 3.4.1.
111. *Ṛgveda*, 1.25.10, 2.28.6, 5.85.1, 6.68.9, 8.42.1; *Artharvaveda*, 6.36.3.
112. *Ṛgveda*, 2.28.1.
113. *Atharvaveda*, 7.12.1., 1.25.1.
114. Chakraborti, *op. cit.*, p.65; Ghurye, G.S., *Vedic* India, p.183; *Satpath Brāhamaṇa*, 5.1.1.13.
115. *Satpath Brāhamaṇ*, 5; *Vājasaini Saṁhita*, 9.10.
116. *Vājsani Saṁhita*, 22, 14; *Satpath Brāhamaṇ*, 13.5.4.21-22; *Taittiriya Brāhmaṇ*, 3.8.
117. *Satpath Brāhamaṇa*, 13.7.1.1,14.
118. Ghosh, R.C., *History of Hindu Civilization*, (Reprint) Delhi, 1985, p.215; Basham, A.L., *op. cit.*, p.140; Clayton A.C., *op. cit.*, p.106.
119. *Sukla Yajurveda Saṁhitā*, 18.15;35.15;40.8; *Atharvaveda* 1.7.6; 20.76.5, 92.14; *Aitereya Brāhamaṇa*, 5.1.27.
120. Kunhanraja. C., *op. cit.* p.165.
121. Pande, G.C., *Bhartiya Parampara kei Mula Svara*, p.44.
122. Dasgupta, Surama, *Development of Moral Philosophy in India*, Delhi, 1994, pp.10-11.
123. Pande, G.C., *op. cit.* p.44; Sinha, A.K., *op. cit.*, p.50.
124. Dasgupta, Surama, *op. cit.*, p.11.
125. *Kathopaniṣad*, 1.2.1-2: cf, Pande, G.C., *op. cit.*, p. 60.
126. Dasgupta, Surama, *op. cit.*, p.12.
127. Similar ideas were reflected in the discussion of Yājñavalkya and his wife Maitreyi in the *Bṛhadāranyaka Upaniṣad*. See, *Bṛhadāraṇyaka Upaniṣad*, 2.4.2-5; Hiriyana, M., *op. cit.*, p.18.
128. Verma, Jaya, *op. cit.*, pp.142-43.
130. In the *Bṛhadāraṇyaka Upaniṣad*, the attitude of Yājñavalkya towards wealth clearly reveals this idea.
131. Sinha, A.K., *op. cit.*, p.51; Verma, Jaya, *op. cit.* p.143.
132. *Bṛhadāraṇyaka Upaniṣad*, 6.4.9, 4.4.10-11, 6.4.20.

133. *Chāndogya Upaniṣad*, 5.11.6.
134. *Maitrayaṇi Upaniṣad*, 3.10.62; Hiriyana, M., *Indian Conception of Values*, p.18.
135. *Kathopaniṣad*, 1.3.10.
136. *Iśa Upaniṣad*, 8.
137. *Praśana Upaniṣad* : 4.5.
138. *Muṇdaka Upaniṣad*, 1.2.12.
139. *ibid*, 3.2.6.
140. *Śvetāśvatara Upaniṣad*, 1.9.
141. *op. cit.*, 4.1.
142. *op. cit.*, 6.23.
143. Sinha, A.K., *op. cit.*, p.51.
144. For different definitions of *Kāma*, see Verma, Jaya, *op. cit.*, pp.73-74.
145. Sinha; A.K., *opcit* p.57, fn.40.
146. Pandey, R.B., *Bhartiya Niti ka Vikas*, p.6.
147. *Vanaparva*, 33.37-38, *Sāntiparva* 13.3.10; Ayer, P.S.S., *Evolution of Hindu Moral Ideals*, Delhi, 1976, p.152.
148. *Vālmiki Rāmāyaṇa, Yudhakand*, Sarga 83, verse 32.
149. Sarga 83 verse 33.
150. Sarga 83 verse 35.
151. Sarga 85 verse 36.
152. *Mahābhārata, Śāntiparva*, 5.8.16, 18,19.
153. *Mahābhārata, Sāntiparava* 5.8.17.
154. *op. cit.*, 5.8.13, 20,21,24.
155. *op. cit.*, 15.48.
156. *op. cit.*, 8.5., 9.34.
157. *op. cit.*, 10.1, 19.4.
158. *op. cit.*, 11.16.
159. *op. cit.*, 18.3, 36., 32, 4.7 64.
160. *op. cit.*, 34.31, 35.10, 47.48.
162. Gupta N.L., *Education and Value in the Mahabharata*, New Delhi, 1995, p.
163. Chakradhar Jha, *History and Sources of Law in Ancient India*, Delhi, 1987. pp. 27-28.
164. *Mahābhārata, Śāntiparva*, chapter 59. Verses, 14, to 29., 35., 80 to 86.
165. *Rāmāyaṇa*, 2.100.4.

166. Samadhar, J.N., *Lectures on the Economic Condition of Ancient India*, 1984, pp.68-70.
167. *Mahābhārata, Śāntiparva*, Chapter 59., verses 80-86.
168. Names of various teachers of *Rājaśāstra* are given in the *Mahābhārata*. Such as *Bṛhaspati, Ausanasa*, Pracesta Manu, *Gaursiras*, etc., see *Śāntiparva*, verses 80-86.
169. Gopal, Lallanji, *Pracina Bhartiya Rajnatik Vicardhara*, p.10.
170. *Kauṭilya Arthaśāstra*, 1.1.
171. *Chande*, M.B., *The Kautalyan Arthaśāstra*, p.2.
172. Jayswal, K.P., *Hindu Polity* Part I p.5.
173. Kangle, R.P., *The Kauṭilya Arthaśāstra*, A study, Part-III, p.1.
174. There is a great controversy over the date of Kauṭilya. All views have their strong and weak points. For different views on the date of Kauṭilya's *Arthaśāstra*. See Jayswal, K.P., *Hindu Polity*, Appendix C p.368-396; Misra, S.C., *Evolution of Kauṭilya's Arthaśāstra* pp.17-47; Kangle, R.P., *The Kauṭilya Arthaśāstra*, Part III A study chapter IV; Drekmeir, C., *Kingship and Community in Early India*, Bombay 1962, pp.192-193, Romila Thapar, *Asoka and Decline of the Mauryas* Delhi 1977, pp.218-227.
175. Roychowdhary, H.C., *Political History of Ancient India*, Calcutta, p.263.
176. Sharma, R.S., *Aspects of Political Ideas and Institutions in Ancient India*, p.22.
177. Chande, M.B., *op. cit.*, p.2.
178. The Phrases like *Raja Kalasya karanam*, etc. are frequently used in the *Māhābharata* and some other texts. Śāntiparva, 67, 72, 73, 79, 91. 6,9, Udyogaparva 132, 16; *Śukranitisāra* 4.1.60; *Kāmandikiya Nitisāra*, 5.82.83; Kane, P.V., *History of Dharamsastra*, (Hindi Tr.), Part II, Lucknow, 1972, p.601-604, 655.
179. *Kauṭilya Arthaśāstra*, 1.3-16-17; Altekar, A.S., *State and Government in Ancient India*, pp.48-49; Sinha A.K., *op. cit.*, pp.136-138.
180. *Kauṭilya Arthaśāstra*, 13.4.5.
181. Sinha, A.K., *op. cit.*, p.53.
182. Roy, B.P., *Later Vedic Economy*, p.118-119.
183. *Taittiriya Saṁhitā*, 1.8.12, *Atharvaveda*, VI 88.2.

184. Sharma, R.S., *op. cit.*, p.273.
185. Verma, Jaya, *Pracina Bharata mein Mulya Cetna aur Artha*, New Delhi, 2001, pp.53.
187. *Canakya Sutra*, 1.88, as quoted by Verma, Jaya, *op. cit.*, p.147.
188. P. Masson Oursel said that *Vṛtti* which is the basis of *Vārta* refers to the whole human activity; *artha* raises the questions of ends, *Vārta* that of means. -Masson, Oursel, P., *Ancient India*, p.106 as quoted by Sinha A.K., *op. cit.*, p.59, fn. 60.
189. Kosambi, D.D., *op. cit.*, p.185-190.
190. Verma, Jaya, *op. cit.*, p.148.
191. Tripathi, P.V., *Purūṣārtha-Catuṣṭaya*, p.233; Kangle, R.P., *op. cit.*-III. p.1.
192. *Kauṭilya Arthaśāstra*, 6.1: Verma, Jaya, *op. cit.*, p.148; Kangle, *op. cit.*, pp.120-2.
193. Ghosh, N.N., *Early History of India*, pp. 279 and ff.
194. Tripathi, H.N., *Pracina Bharat Mein Rajya aur Nyayapalika*, p.22.
195. Sinha, A.K., *op. cit.*, p.59. fn. 65.
196. Sinha, A.K., *opcit*, p.54.
197. *Kauṭilya Arthaśāstra*, 1.3.16.17,17,1.4.16.
198. Sinha, A.K., *op. cit.*, p.54.
199. Yadava, B.N.S., *Presidential Address.* Ancient India section, *Proceedings of Indian History Congress*, Bombay 1980, p.23; also Verma, Jaya, *op. cit.*, p.149.
200. Sharma, R.S., *Indian Feudalism*, (Hindi Tr.), Delhi, 1973, pp. 3-5.
201. Sinha, A.K., *op. cit.*, p.54.
202. *Amarkośa*, III-3-86.
203. *Kāmandaka Nitisāra;* 3.629; 4.7.64.77; 5.8.16, 63,66,76,83,88; 9.14.14-7.
204. *Ibid*, p.4.62.
205. *Śukranitisāra* 4.356.
206. *Śukranitisāra* 4.3.177.
207. *Ibid*, 4.3.176.
208. *Bṛhaspati Sūtra*, 6.7.12.
209. *Manusmṛti* 2.224.
210. *Kāmasūtra* 1.20.
211. Devraj, N.K., op. cit.,107-108.

212. Raghuvamsa, 17.65, 5.8, 16.2, 17.64, 17.66.
213. *Kiratarjuniyam* of Bharvi as quoted by Devraja, N.K., *The Mind and Spirit of India*, p.106.
214. *Subhasita-ratna bhandgara* (Nirnaya Sagar Press, 1989) p.62, Quoted by Devraja, N.K., *op. cit.*, p.106.
215. *Nitiśatakam*, "यस्याति वित्त स नरः कुलीनः"
216. *Ibid*, 42.

3. *Artha* and *Arthaśāstra*

Every culture possesses its own value-system exhibited through the way of life, philosophy, law, social and cultural traditions prevalent in it.[1] This gives culture a distinct identity from the other ones.[2] Primarily Indian culture is thought to be a value-based spiritual culture. Therefore, all notions, beliefs, terms and concepts, etc. developed in it are influenced directly or indirectly with this spiritualism possessing a close relationship with each other. No doubt this spiritualism is the ethos of Indian culture[3] and due to this, Indian culture has often been treated as a culture having world negating attitude and Indians as possessing on desire for material and empirical achievements of life.[4] But making an in-depth enquiry into the nature of Indian culture and way of life, this seems to be a mis-conception only. Ancient Indians had, no less, possessed a positive and world-affirming attitude since the beginning of their culture[5] and they had developed a clear-cut thinking on the matter other than the spiritual attainments.[6] Instead of giving emphasis on either of the two attitudes (i.e., world affirmative or world-negating) Indian culture advocates a harmony between the spiritual and material achievements. This idea is best represented in the concept of *Purūṣārtha-Catuṣṭay* which is a synthesis of material, moral and spiritual values.[7] *Artha*, in this scheme of four-fold values, stands for material and empirical value that is essential for man's survival, thus, appears before us as a value of life. It is for this reason only that *artha* in ancient Indian value system, as already stated in previous chapter, is a notion which, primarily, is used to denote value-in-general hence *arthaśāstra* stands for the science of value (*artha* being the value and śāstra being the science). Both these notions possess a wider significance in ancient India but nowadays they are generally taken to denote politico-economic value and science of polity and statecraft respectively. These conceptions could develop mainly due to the famous treatise of Kauṭilya bearing the same title that deals with topics related to matters of polity and statecraft. In his *Arthaśāstra*, Kauṭilya defined *artha* and *arthaśāstra* in a technical sense, viz., *artha* as livelihood of man and inhabited land and *arthaśāstra* as a science of maintaining and protecting that earth.[8] As *artha* in Kautiliyan terminology is a politico-economic value. Hence *arthaśāstra* is the science of polity and statecraft. *Arthaśāstra* is related to inseparably with *artha* and it literally means the science of *artha*.[9] Therefore, with the changing connotations of *artha*, the connotation of *arthaśāstra* changed accordingly. In its wider connotation *arthaśāstra* is a science of value and along with matters of polity and statecraft covers all those things that are related to *artha* as value-in-general. In this way *arthaśastra* is the science of value that is transformed into science of polity in Kauṭiliyan period and as the science of wealth is post-Kauṭiliyan period.

How and why this broader notion of *arthaśāstra* transformed into a narrow meaning of science of wealth, will be the point of discussion in this chapter. Keeping in view this objective the origin and development of the *arthaśāstra* will be discussed in the forthcoming lines and an attempt will be carried out to analyze those changes that have occurred in the notion of *arthaśāstra* due to the changing notions of *artha*. With the historical and cultural development of the country, many changes occurred in the notion of *artha*. They definitely influenced for a change in the notion of *arthaśāstra* too. The discussion will be made after through keeping a close eye on the historical development of India and an effort will also be made to relate those changes in the notion of *arthaśāstra* to the changes that occurred in the ideological and political sphere of the country.

The historical period of India dates from Ṛgvedic age, and as already said *artha* has been used in a variety of senses in this Veda. In its different usages such as purpose,[10] aim,[11] goal,[12] object,[13] wish,[14], end,[15] wealth,[16] etc. It stands for material and empirical gain. So for the early Aryans, '*artha*', as indicated from these usages, was value-in-general and was a medium through which they could achieve pleasure and comfort.[17] In this form it was the most desirable value for them. In this period, as reflected from some early passages, the culture and society of the Aryans was in rudimentary stage. They were trying to be settling in a new atmosphere. Their social traditions, customs, laws, etc. were not yet fully developed. The roots of all those notions and concepts such as *varṇa*, *dharma*, *artha*, *kāma*, state, etc.[18] which later on became most influential in Indian culture and society, could be traced in this Veda, though in that period they had not acquired their definite form. They were also in the rudimentary form. The serious thinking on all these notions was not developed yet. In this early phase Aryans were making adjustments with the new atmosphere and as they were living in the pastoral and tribal phase of their culture,[19] they did not even feel the need of serious thinking of all these notions. Their society was small with less socio-economic and moral problems that could be solved easily without much pain. So there was a lack of serious thinking on all these aspects of life and society in the early phase of *Ṛgveda*. In the later phase as reflected through some late passages of *Ṛgveda*, Aryans settled down permanently in the country. The tribal phase of their culture came to an end and they diverted their attention towards other things.[20] There was a gradual growth in the society of Aryans which certainly gave rise to some moral as well socio-economic problems. It seems that now they might felt the need of serious thinking, individually on each and every aspect of life which later on gave rise to the systematic study of different *śāstras*. This does not imply that we have any skeptic view regarding the intellectual genius of early Aryans. We, certainly, admit that there was no dearth of intellectual consciousness in early Aryans as evident from various hymns in which serious aspects of life and society such as creation of world, *yajña*, *dharma*, *ṛta*, *varṇa*, etc.[21] were discussed very efficiently. We want to highlight here only that there was a lack of systematization and consistency in their ideas which is the basic pre-requisite of a *śāstra*. Therefore, there was less possibility of development of institutionalized branches of learning in this early age.[22] The unification of these ideas in the form of a *śāstra* seems to be an advancement of later Vedic age that witnessed many significant changes in the life and society of Aryans.

On social level the idea of class structure *Varṇa-Vyavasthā*[23] was developed as revealed from the *Pūruṣa-Sūkta* of *Ṛgveda* in which for the first time the idea of four-fold division of society was reflected. This system of *Varṇa-Vyavasthā* on the one hand systematized and classified the whole Aryan society into four *varṇas* and on the other hand gave rise to many social inequalities as later on this system became very rigid and in place of occupation one's *varṇa* was decided on the basis of birth. This gave birth to the system of hierarchy in social order as a result of which social inequalities increases as social importance of a Brāhmaṇ or a Kṣatriya was much more than a Vaiśya or a śudra.[24] On the political level, the process of territorial state formation which had already begun in early days, culminated[25] and it transformed the tribal-rural *Jana* of Ṛgvedic age into rural-urban *Janapadas* with vast territory and protecting and increasing of this territory became the ambition of ruling class. This age witnessed the growth of imperialistic tendencies as reflected from various titles[26] that were used in later Vedic texts[27] for the king and his power. The king was the head of the state[28] but for maintaining and controlling state affairs he was in need of assistance of other people. This requirement gave birth to administrative system which was in practice, exercised through bureaucrats responsible to ministers appointed by the king. Though in early Vedic period also administrative system was prevalent as there were references to assemblies and ministers that used to assist the *Janapati* in maintaining the state affairs.[29] The change that occurred in the later Vedic period was that in this period there recorded a gradual growth in the number and power of *Ratnins*[30] which clearly indicate that the population of the Aryans was also increased and to maintain order in the society *Janapati* or king need more officials.

On economic level also many changes occurred. The center of economic activity was shifted from cattle-rearing to agriculture.[31] The later Vedic period witnessed the growth of an agriculture-based economy in which land was highly important. In the later Vedic texts there are several passages[32] which shows that there was a gradual growth in the importance of land and it was regarded as a 'mother'. The Pṛthvi-Sūkta of *Atharva Veda* was a good example of this thinking in which land had been regarded as a mother and was taken as the giver of all kinds of wealth.[33] Owing to this, land became highly important and thus turned into a principal cause of conflicts between *janapadas*, as they could become prosperous through acquiring more and more land.

In religious sphere also, many new changes occurred.

The performance of sacrifices that was quite easy in the Ṛgvedic period was transformed into a highly complex and ritualistic affair[34] and only experts in that rituals could perform them. Thus simplicity replaced complexity in *Yajñas.*[35] This complexity of performing *Yajñas* rituals resulted in the enhancement of the social prestige of Brāhmaṇas as they were experts in performing these rituals.[36] This supremacy of Brāhmaṇas later on challenged by many religious movements that arose in retaliation.

All these developments contributed to the growth of Indian culture on one hand but on the other hand they paved the way for many socio-economic, religious and moral problems which certainly required solutions. A desire of solving these problems arose as the main cause for the growth of serious thinking on each and every aspect of life and society. Therefore in this age we find that various *śāstras* were originated. It seems that about "8th century B.C.", as Altekar holds, "an age of specialization commenced and the specialists in grammar and etymology, prosody and astronomy began to form separate schools and composed special manuals for the beginners as well as for the advanced scholars".[37] So it seems that in this age, special schools for each separate branch of learning replaced the ancient Vedic school and that the school of *arthaśāstra* could rise and become impetuous in passing years resulting in its general acceptance as an independent branch of learning.[38]

From 8th to 6th Century B.C. India, witnessed the rise and growth of various philosophical schools[39] that held diverse view regarding life, world and absolute reality. Among these schools, there was a school of *lokāyatas* which was materialist in nature and utilitarian in approach.[40] *Lokāyatas* declared *artha* and *kāma* as the only values of life[41] and discarded all other values. Their philosophy put its emphasis on the development of *arthaśāstra* whose subject-matter was classifyging.[42] In this period the subject matter of different branches of learning was classifying. The *sastra* dealing with moral and legal ideas was called *Dharamśāstra.*[43] *Moksaśāstra* dealt with the spiritual ideas.[44] When the science of wealth, property and livelihood was classified as a branch of learning, it was called *Vārta.*[45] The science dealing with governing state and policy was called *Dandaniti.*[46] The means of livelihood are socially organized resources for the support and fulfilment of life. Thus the means of livelihood was needed to be regulated by the state in public interest. So there may prevail security and welfare in the society. *Vārta* was the science of economic policy used by state. It was integrated with *dandaniti* in the later period and this integrated form gave birth to *arthaśāstra.*[47] After this development, *arthaśāstra* came to be used mainly for polity and statecraft which was also known as *Nitiśāstra,*[48] *Dandanitiśāstra, Rājanitiśāstra, Rājadharma, Rājyasaśtrā, Nṛpaśāstra.*[49] Though in technical sense, *arthaśāstra* is some what wider in meaning than *dandaniti* or *rājaniti* and include politics, economics, law, and justice.[50] With regard to its origin nothing can be said with certainty. In the Purāṇas[51] it was said to be an *upaveda* of *Atharvaveda* but how and when this *śāstra* originated in India and who were its earliest exponents can't be said with certainty. Like other branches of knowldege a mythological origin of *Arthaśāstra* was discussed in the chapter 59 of the *Śāntiparvan* of the *Mahābhārata.* According to it, in the beginning there was Kṛtayuga, people acted according to the rules of *dharma* and their was neither ruler nor punishment.[52] Later on during the course of time, delusion, greed, love of pleasures, and other passions were developed which resulted in a state of anarchy.[53] Seeing this state of society the gods were filled with sadness and approached to *Brahmā*, the Creator and requested him to find the way out.[54] For guiding the conduct of the people Brahmadeva wrote a detailed treatise of one hundred thousand chapters which dealt with *trivarga* (*Dharma-artha-kāma*) and four lores (*Trayi*, *Ānvikṣiki*, *Vārta* and *Dandaṇiti*)[55] and this work was named as *Daṇdanti*.[56] As it was a colossal work it was first abridged by Viśālakṣa, i.e. God Śiva in ten thousand chapters and it was thus called *Viśālakṣa śāstra*.[57] Śiva was followed by Bahudanta or Indra who reduced it further into five thousand chapters and his treatise was known as *Bahudantaśāstra*. After Indra, Bṛhaspati abridged it in 3000 chapters and it was called *Bārhaspatya śāstra*. Finally it was abridged by Uśanasa into one thousand chapters and his treatise was known as *Auśanasaśāstra*.[58] Though it is purely a mythological account but it clearly depicts that tradition of *arthaśāstra* was prevalent in India from very ancient times. Along with this, the *Mahābhārata* also gives the names of the seven promulgators of *Rājyaśastra*, i.e. *Rājyaśāstra praṇetarah*. These are Bṛhaspati, Kāvya (Uśanasa) Viśālakṣa, Mahendra (Indra), Prācetas Manu, Bhāradvaja and Gaursiras.[59] Kauṭilya also refered to them in his *Arthaśāstra*[60] but as their treatise were not available we can't say anything regarding their teachings. But these references clearly testify the antiquity of this *śāstra*. But it is difficult to give a precise date for the origin of this *śāstra* in India. We also have no concrete idea about its earliest exponents. On the basis of available sources the beginning of political awareness in India could be traced back to Ṛgvedic period.[61] In the *Ṛgveda*, political society had been regarded as a big family[62] and this relation of king and subjects became an ideal for the theories of Indian polity in later centuries. Various passages of *Ṛgveda* reveal that Aryans possessed awareness regarding political speculation, for instance at one place, it is said that it is the duty of the king to punish the wretched for the security of the subjects.[63] At another place, it is said that as father looks after his son, *Tejasvin* king should also do so. People should afraid of him.[64] The foremost work of the king was to maintain peace and order in the society. So in the Ṛgvedic period also a positive structure of political body was speculated, people started to think over the matters of politics but their thinking was in the form of scattered and thin ideas. It seems that like other branches of knowledge science of polity also acquired a definite shape in the later Vedic period. Altekar holds that the science of polity has acquired an independent status near about 6th century B.C.,[65] while Drekmeier is of opinion that it was around 7th century B.C.,[66] that politics was studied in India as an independent branch of learning. Bhandarkar is of the opinion that *Arthaśāstra* occupied an independent status in 650 B.C.[67]

In this connection Pant[68] have attracted our attention towards the *Kṣtra-Vidyā* mentioned in the *Chāndogya Upaniṣad* in the list of branches of knowledge prevailed at that time.[69] In this *Upaniṣad, Kṣtravidya* is mentioned along with four Vedas, *Itihāsa-Purāna, Rāsi, Naksatra Vidyā, Bhuta Vidyā, Sarpa-Vidyā, Deva-Vidyā, Brahma-Vidyā, Tana-Vidyā,* etc. Some of these branches of learning were old and already known[70] but most of the branches were new and not mentioned in the earlier texts. As said earlier, this period (8th-7th century B.C.) was a very fertile period in the intellectual sphere of the country and as a result of intellectual activities many new branches of learning were developed and systematic study started in the existing branches. It may be assumed safely that it is quite possible that along with other *śastras, arthaśāstra,* was also developed in this age only. Pant hold that initially, *arthaśāstra* was *Kṣtra-Vidyā* which was a *mantra,* i.e. worldly knowledge,[71] distinct from *Ātma-Vidyā.*[72] But what the exact connotation of the term was not clearly mentioned in the *Chandogya Upanisad.* Moreover details regarding its subject matter were also not available. Though the term was mentioned by Pāṇini[73] as well as Patanjali.[74]

Śankaracārya took it as a synonym of *Dhanur-Veda* and scholars like Keith,[75] Hopkins followed this meaning.[76] V.S. Agarwal[77] and B.C. law[78] called it a military science. Pant took it as to mean a body of practical maxims on state affairs on the basis of Pali Cannon and Jātakas.[79] Aryasura (4th century A.D.) in his *Jātaka Māla* used term *Rājdharma* and *Kṣtravidyā* as synonymous in the sense of royal duties.[80] Buddhagosha in *Visuddhimagga* (5th century A.D.) understood *Kṣtravidyā* as science of polity (*niti sattam*).[81] In the Jātaka tales there were many references which shows that politics had become a general topic of discussion. It is called *khattivijja* or *khat dharma* though in most of the cases it was regarded as a false and immoral science, thus, was condemned. *Jātakas* like *Mahābodhi*, *Mahā Sutasoma*, *Mahāumagga*, etc. unanimously condemned this science.[82] *Milindpañho* holds that the knowledge of *Khatta dharma* was given to the prince[83] which includes in it art of war and knowledge of administration and law.[84]

The terms *Kṣtra* and *kṣātradharma* both appears in the *Rāmāyaṇa* also. In this epic also these were condemned and *Rāmāyaṇa* regards *Kṣtravidyā* as *anārya mattih* which should never took as his guide by a person who wished to follow the path of right.[85] *Ksātradharma* was also regarded by *Rāmāyaṇa* as *adharma*. It is said that it is *dharma* of name only and was followed by the people who were low, greedy and were engaged in sinful acts.[86]

Kṣtra-vidyā is also mentioned in the chapter XII of the *Māhabhārata*. While discussing the policy to be adopted by a king who was surrounded by enemies it is advised that he should follow '*Kṣtra-vidyā*'[87] like rat Palita.[88] On the basis of above discussion it seems that probably Pant was quite right in his view and *Kṣtra-vidyā* was probably the science of polity and statecraft in which subjects regarding royal duties were studied. U.N. Ghosal,[89] B.M. Barua,[90] R.L. Mehta[91] also used the term in the same sense. R.K.

Mookherjee has also taken the meaing of this term as the science of ruling class. i.e. science of polity or administration.[92] Ghosal on the basis of Pali Cannons and Jātakas holds that "Kṣatriya science is...concerned to be a systematic body of knowledge which we may identify for all practical purpose with *Arthaśāstra* (or more generally 'the science of politics')"[93]

So it may be safely concluded as Pant holds that the origin of *Arthaśāstra* could be ascribed to the same period to which early Upaniṣads belong.[94] Up to this period sciences such as phonetics, etymology, grammar and metrics had already developed into independent disciplines. As till this period big states were also came into existence and kings were in need of some branch of learning on the matter of polity and statecraft. So all political and intellectual changes that had taken place in the ancient India clearly, present the evidence of the fact that a body of knowledge dealing with statecraft and duties of king must have come into existence till this period. It may have been denoted by any of terms either *Rājdharma*,[95] *Kṣtravidyā*,[96] *Rājavidyā*[97] or *Arthaśāstra*.[98] As in this age political power became more important, therefore, *arthaśāstra* with the mingling of the ideas of *Vārta* and *Dandaniti* acquired a new form and transformed into the science of polity and statecraft. Who were the real exponents of this science is not clearly mentioned. Though on the basis of the *Mahābhārata* and *Arthaśāstra* it seems that there was a good tradition of this learning and not less than five schools and thirteen individuals contributed in the growth of this science in pre-Kautiliyan period. These are Bṛhaspati, Uśanasa, Mānava, Āmbiyas, Parāsara, Bhārdvāja, Piṣun, Kaunapadant, Vātavyādhi, Bahudantiputram, Ghotamukha, Kātyāyan, Cāryana,[99] etc. But as their treatises are not available today we cannot say anything with certainty regarding their teachings.

The earliest extant work available on this śāstra was the *Arthaśāstra* of Kauṭilya which deals with the matters of polity and statecraft. There is a big controversy regarding the date of *Arthaśāstra* of Kauṭilya. While the traditional view supported by Shamasastri,[100] Ganapatisastri,[101] N.N. Law,[102] V.A. Smith,[103] Fleet,[104] K.P. Jayaswal,[105] J.J. Meyers,[106] N.C. Bandopadhyaya,[107] R.K. Mookerjee,[108] F.W. Thomas,[109] D.R. Bhandarkar,[110] V.R. Ramchandra Dikshitar,[111] P.V. Kane,[112] R.G. Basak,[113] D.D. Kosambi,[114] B. Breloer,[115] K.A. Nilakanthasastri,[116] R.P. Kangle,[117] etc. holds that it was written by Cāṇakya, the minister of Candragupta Maurya and belong to fourth century B.C. This traditional view is reinforced by the fact that a statement about the authorship of the work is found in the first chapter, where towards the end it is stated that the *śāstra* was composed by Kauṭilya avoiding all prolixity, etc.[118] At the end of the work it is stated that that person who in resentment rescued the earth from the Nanda kings composed this *śastra.*[119] The tradition that Kauṭilya was the author of *Arthaśāstra* seems to be generally accepted from very ancient time. Reference to *Arthaśāstra* and Kauṭilya are found in many sources. Kamandaka asserts in his *Nitisara* that the wise Viṣṇugupta who had destroyed the Nandas by his magic lore and given the earth to Candragupta had extracted the nectar of Nitisāra from the ocean of *Arthaśāstra.*[120] Dandin in his *Daśa kumār carita* ascribes *Arthaśāstra* to Kauṭilya that he composed it for the sake of Mauryan king.[121] Viṣṇu Sharma, the author of *Pañcatantra* also ascribed the *Arthaśāstra* to Kauṭilya. Bāṇabhatta was aware of the treatise wrote by Kauṭilya.[122] The *Arthaśāstra* is referred to in the *Nitivākyamrta* of Somadeva, *Kathāsarita sāgar* and the *Nandisūtra.* It is also said by scholars that Vātsyāyan modeled his work on the *Arthaśāstra* and both Kālidāsa and Yājñavalkya seem to be indebted to Kauṭilya's work. The society which Manu and Yājñavalkya depicted was of later period than that one which Kauṭilya had portrayed in his *Arthaśāstra*. The civil and constitutional law explained by Kauṭilya and Megeasthenes were the same.[123]

This traditional view is contested by many scholars such as J. Jolly,[124] Hillebrandt,[124A] M. Winternitz,[125] A.B. Keith,[126] O. Stein,[127] E.H. Johnston, R.G. Bhandarkar, Kalidas Nag,[128] Pran Nath,[129] H.C. Raychaudhuri,[130] Atindranath Bose,[131] S.C. Misra[132] and others. But these scholars hold no single view regarding any possible date of *Arthaśāstra*. H.C. Raychaudhri and A.N. Bose prefers to place it in or about first century A.D., Johnston places it near about 250 A.D.[133] Keith holds that it was written in 300 A.D. Jolly believes that the work might have been composed in the third century A.D. R.G. Bhandarkar considers the first or second century A.D. to be the earliest date that can be referred to Kauṭilya.[134] S.C. Misra proposed that some passages of *Arthaśāstra* could be dated up to 12 century A.D. So scholars who opposed traditional view possessed no unanimous opinion regarding the date of *Arthaśāstra*, Remarking on this Raychowdhry writes, "The *Arthaśāstra* certainly existed before Bāṇa (seventh century A.D.), the *Nandisutra* of the jains (not later than the fifth century A.D.) and possibly Jātakmālā of Aryasura (third or fourth century A.D.). In the Junagarh rock inscription of Skandagupta reference is made to testing officials by *upadhas*, as we find in the *Arthaśāstra*. The prevalence of the study of *Arthavidyā* in still earlier days is proved by the Junagarh rock inscription of Rudradaman I which mentions such technical terms as *pranaya*, *visti*, etc. which might have been derived from Kauṭilya itself".[135] Though there is no end of the controversy and modern scholars do not and probably will never agree on the date of *Arthaśāstra*. But a compromise is suggested by Basham who holds that "yet it is certainly pre-Guptan and we believe the elaboration of a Mauryan original which was perhaps the work of Kauṭilya himself".[136]

In the period of Mauryas India for the first time witnessed political unity. The founder of the dynasty Candragupta Maurya brought the vast area of the country under his rule and rest was annexed by Aśoka. With the foundation of this empire imperialistic tendencies that have started in later Vedic age achieved its climax.

Kauṭilya was the minister of Candragupta Maurya and as tradition spoke he guided the latter during his conquests. The task before Kauṭilya was to protect this newly founded empire. As a statesman he was wise enough to realize that without having a strong administration, empire could not survive. So to guide the emperor on the matters of polity and statecraft he wrote a practical testimony. He used *artha* in the definite sense of subsistence and inhabited land. In fact it was the earth that contained men and therefore, *Arthaśāstra*, according to him, was the science that dealt with the acquisition and protection of the earth.[137] A state could be regarded, as a state when it contained inhabited land or territory. It was only from this inhabited territory that a state could get manpower that was an important resource.[138] Keeping this view in mind he used the word '*artha*' in a very technical sense. As *arthaśāstra* was the science that dealt with the acquisition and preservation of the earth which in fact were the method of administration, thus, Kauṭilya used *Arthaśāstra* significantly in the sense of science of statecraft and polity.

The *Arthaśāstra* of Kauṭilya is an excellent treatise on the matters of polity and statecraft. It is divided into fifteen *adhikarans*. Book-I deals with the equipment of the king for the performance of his duties as ruler and discusses topics like training of the king, the appointment of ministers and other officials of state and so on. Book-II principally describes the details of the various executive officers of the state. It furnishes a comprehensive account of the state activities in various fields, including a discourse on such questions as settlement of unoccupied land, building a fort, laying out the capital, etc. Book-III is mainly concerned with law and order and its administration. It, thus, reproduces a complete code of law. Book-IV describes how the crime should be suppressed. It guided one about the tracing, tracking and punishment of the thieves, murderers, dacoits and other criminals. Book-V deals with miscellaneous aspects such as measures that may be necessary in emergencies, and steps to be taken against seditious persons. It also lays down scales of salaries for different categories of state servants. It also explains how a candidate for a high office should endeavour to secure and retain it. It also gives advice to chief minister on ensuring continuity of rule on the demise of ruling monarch. Book-VI enumerates the qualities necessary to make each of the seven constituents of the state ideal. It also describes *mandala* theory as a preliminary a discussion on the states relations with its neighbours. Book-VII discusses elaborately the measures of foreign policy. Book-VIII is concerned with calamities, shortcomings, or weakness affecting the various constituents of the state. Book-IX deals with preparation of war, and describes the kinds of troops that could be mobilized for an expedition, the proper season for the start of an expedition and the precaution to be takes and inherent dangers to be guarded against, before starting the expedition etc. Book-X describes the various methods of warfare. It also describes the battle array and even petty matters relating to camping ground, and such allied topics. Book-XI deals with the republics and methods that a conquerer could use to subjugate them. Book-XII depicts a weak king, when threatened by a strong king, should frustrate the ambition of that king and ultimately overcome him. Book-XIII is concerned mainly with the conquest of enemy's fortified capital. It also describes how the conquered territory should be ruled by the conqueror. Book-XIV deals with the various secret remedies and practices those are useful for getting rid of enemies or traitors prone to indulge in committing or adopting treachery. Finally, Book-XV describes and illustrates from the text itself the thirty two *tantrayuktis* or methods of treating a subject.[139]

Kauṭilya, thus, gave new dimensions to the science of *artha*. "The *Arthaśāstra* of Kauṭilya represented thc high water mark of the science of polity." The tradition of polity that was prevailing in India achieved its culmination in this treatise. The first instance of *Arthaśāstra* in the form of science of polity,[140] all though, can be traced in the *Mahābhārata*, but the roots of this tradition (i.e. *arthaśāstra* in the form of science of polity) could be traced earlier. As the *Rajdharma* was regarded as an important subject, therefore, all the Dharamśāstra writers dealt it in a great deal.

Kamasutra also gave a similar story regarding the origin of *Arthaśāstra*. According to it Prajapati wrote a detailed treatise of one-lakh chapters, which was summarized by Manu as *Dharamśāstra*, Bṛhaspati as *Arthaśāstra*, Nandi as *Kamaśāstra*.[141] Apastamba *Dharamsūtra* indicated towards the *Arthaśāstra*. *Niti prākāśika* also tells that Brhama, Mahesvara, Skandha, Indra, Pracetasa Manu, Bṛhaspati, Sukra, Bhārdvaja, Vedavyās and Gaursiras, were the exponents of *Rājdharma*, who had abridged the treatise of science of polity wrote by Brahma and called them '*Rājaśāstranāma Prānetah*'. Extending the details of the *Mahābhārata* it tells that Gaursira and Vedvyās, further abridged it into five hundred and three hundred chapters respectively.[142] Asvaghosha also gave their names in the *Buddha Carita*.[143] In the very first sloka of the *Pañcatantra*, Manu, Bṛhaspati, Śukra, Parāśara and his son, Cāṇakya, etc. has been referred to as authors of *Nṛpa-Sāstra*.[144] *Mitākṣara*, the commentary, on Yājṇavalkya has also taken the *Daṇdaniti* in the sense of *arthaśāstra*. All these instances clearly reveal that the tradition of *Arthaśāstra* as a science of polity had known from or early date but it received maturity in the *Arthaśāstra* of Kauṭilya.

As mature stage of any branch of learning presupposes some preliminary stages because without having some initial stages maturity cannot be achieved. As Kauṭilya's treatise shows the culmination of science of polity and statecraft in India, it can automatically be taken that there had been a line of thought in this branch of learning, though, it would not have had a definite form or shape, This also becomes clear from the very first *sūtra* of Kauṭilya's *Arthaśāstra* where he clearly declares his *Arthaśāstra* as compendium, written after compiling all the *arthaśāstra* composed by the earlier masters. Though we do not have any definite information regarding these earlier masters yet this *sūtra* of *Arthaśāstra* clearly indicates that prior to Kauṭilya there was a rich tradition of polity and statecraft in India. As we have no texts available of this science prior to the time of Kauṭilya, it would be difficult to say anything with certainty about the then personalities and the compositions of those acāryas. This tradition of *arthaśāstra*, after Kauṭilya appears to have stagnated and declined. As after the decline of Mauryan Empire, tendencies of decentralization prevailed. Due to the absence of any centralized power, individuality prevailed in every sphere. The branch of learning, like *arthaśāstra* which prominently was dealing with the matters of state certainly faced a setback. As state was not remained so strong to extend all the privileges, peace and security to its subjects, thus feelings of individuality prevailed that gave birth to individual ownership of land,[145] in place of Kauṭilya's ideal of state ownership. So this science of polity and statecraft stagnated and decline up to this stage that no one cared to preserve its ancient literature and all ancient literature on the subject lost.[146] This literature was available in the period of Kauṭilya as he referred to the opinion of ancient teachers at many places. But after the period of Kauṭilya we did not find the reference of any of the ancient texts.

This tradition was declined to such an extent that many centuries after Kauṭilya nothing was wrote on the subject. But before Kauṭilya the science prevailed in India in full swing. The reason of this is also inherent in the historical-cultural-social atmosphere of the country. From the *Ṛgvedic* period to period of Kauṭilya the process of state building was in progress. As Vedic people sought the moral basis of every aspect of life, thus, the political authority was also regarded as the earthly conforming of the authority of Indra and Varuṇa. (The ruler of gods and the protector of *Ṛta* respectively).[147] This relationship between Indra and Varuna was expressed ritually. Order was *kstra* and power was divine and there relationship with one another was expressed as a marriage of sacerdotium (*Brahma*) and the Regnum (*Kstra*).[148] On the earthly level purohit class represented sacerdotium and warrior class represented the Regnum, thus a close relationship between royalty and priesthood is assumed in Vedic India. In fact "the two were regarded as complementary orders because ultimately authority implies the union of will and knowledge".

In the later Vedic period, it was clearly accepted that the ultimate source of authority is law (*daṇda*).[149] The importance of law was detailed in the *Dharamśāstra.*[150] But this law on the temporal level was "related to and interpreted by the Brāhmaṇ." But Kṣatriyas were assigned the duty of enforcing this law.[151] The ultimate source of authority in the Vedic age was law and it was manifested on the earth through Brāhmaṇ and Kṣatriya.

In the sixth and fifth centuries B.C., India witnessed the growth of imperialistic tendencies. To conquer new and new territories was the ambition of the ruling class. This ambition led to series of war and conquest between different states of this period. Professional administrators and soldiers accompanied these political adventures. All these things resulted in the change of the position of social classes. The ruling class was now held in a more high esteem and for them "the state was essentially a structure of power rather than that of moral obligations."[152] It was now held widely that the important source of the political power was military force accompanied by the wealth, policy and public opinion, which could be changed. All these developments also led to a change in the nature of objective to be pursued by state now in place of *dharma*, *artha* was regarded as objective of the state. As the class of professional administrators was emerged and nature and scope of state policy was changed largely, the idea of *rājdharma* was also charged. *Rājdharma*, mainly, stands for the duties of the king. In the early age king was the source of authority because state was small and he could manage its affairs easily. Owing to this reason we found that in later Vedic period he was regarded as the head of judicial and financial administration. These duties of the king were included in the *Rājdharma*. But when the size of the state was increased the old idea of *Rājdharma* that reflected the idea of moral obligations decreased. In place of *Rājdharma*, *daṇdaniti* became the objective of state policy.

As *niti* relates means to end, thus, *daṇdaniti* was that branch of learning which related "the power as means to the attainment of ends" which now was "conceived as *artha* or as *trivarga*." In the Śāntiparva of the *Mahābhārata* we find many instances, which shows that attempts to justify this form of political power was going on. In the Bhiṣma-Yudhiṣthira dialogue, Bhiṣma clearly said that "well-employed and equitable *daṇda* protects the people, it is the same as *dharma*." "*Daṇda* is divine (*daivam hi paramodaṇdah*)."[153]

In the *Arthaśāstra* of Kauṭilya there are references of

schools of political thought, which "regarded religion and morality as only a cloak to be used by the ruler to his own advantage."[154]

In the period preceding Kauṭilya, political power was raised to the prime position. As Kauṭilya was the minister of the integrated empire of Mauryas he naturally, adopted measures that could establish, this empire on more sound foundations. So he gave *arthaśāstra* a new dimension. After Kauṭilya, no centralized political power left in the country and it was only after four-five centuries that we found the centralized power in northern India in the form of Gupta Empire. In between these Kuṣāṇas, Sakas established their kingdoms but they were not lasted long. So this tradition of political thoughts declined significantly in absence of any strong centralized power. When Guptas again established the powerful kingdom this tradition was once again revived in the writings of Kāmandaka, and in post-Gupta period through Somadeva, Brhatrhari, Hemcandra, and Śukra.

Kāmandaka in some matters, such as education, *prakrtis*, *mandala*, expressed new ideas.[155] Through the writings of Kāmandaka the tradition of *artha* continued once again but the change, which occurred in it, was that he wrote only a theoretical book on the subject while the treatise of Kauṭilya was the example of theory and practice. In the period of Kāmandaka there was a complete disintegration between theory and practice.[156] What Kāmandaka wrote was not is the practice. Same trend continued in the writings of Somadeva and Brhathari who, though in definition used old theory and made no attempts to review it in reference to the changing situation in the political atmosphere and this age witnessed "a virtual reduction of the science to the unprincipled principle of expediency for all practical purposes and the older science was lost in course of time."[157] *Artha* till now come to be used significantly for wealth and *arthaśāstra* was the science that dealt with the matter of earning wealth. It is in this sense Śukra in his '*Nitisara*' used it.[158] As in Gupta and post-Gupta period the idea of *Dharma-vijay* was more prevalent than the *Dig-Vijay*, thus, a feudal-federal political structure evolved in which individual wealth was more important. Therefore, the tradition of *Arthaśāstra* as science of polity ceased and it now transformed into the science of wealth and was used significantly in this sense in the later period.

It is quite clear from the above description that the tradition of *Arthaśāstra* in ancient India was a tradition of values, though its connotation and scope changed with historical changes. But in all its connotation, i.e. the science of value to the science of wealth, it reflected the idea of value but revealed a gradual decrease in its scope and at last it came to denote a much narrow conception of science of wealth much because of the reason that with the development of the notion of *Purūṣārtha*, all the values of life were merged in it. As *artha* in this scheme stands for material possession and later on this meaning of *artha* remained continued and hence *arthaśāstra* became the science of wealth.

NOTES AND REFERENCES

1. Taylor defined "Culture as a complex whole that includes all things into one". *Primitive Culture*, p.1; Devraj, N.K., *Samskrti Kei Darsanika Vivecana*, Lucknow, 1972, pp.171-172; Sinha, A.K., *op. cit.*, p.60.
2. Sinha, A.K., "On the problem of cultural identity with special reference to Ancient Indian and Greek cultures." in *Graco-Indica Demetrius Galanos Memorial Volume* (ed.) U.P. Arora, Delhi, 1989, pp. 280-81.
3. Radha Krishnan, S., *Indian Philosophy*, Vol-I, pp.24-25.
4. Max Muller very aptly said that "to the Greek, existence is full of life and reality, to the Hindus it is a dream, an illusion".

History of Sanskrit Literature, p.18.

5. Radha Krishnan, S., *The Spirit of Religion*, Delhi, 1978, p.59; Murty, K.Sachidananda, *The Indian Spirit*, Waltair, 1965, pp.41, 102.
6. Basham, A.L., *The Wonder that was India*, p.79.
7. Gupta Shanti Nath, *Indian Concept of Values*, p.1.
8. *The Kauṭilya Arthaśāstra*, (ed.) R.P. Kangle Part-1, p.15.
9. Kane, P.V., *History of Dharamsastra*, Vol-1 p.151.
10. *Ṛgveda*, 1.124; 2.39.1.
11. *Ibid*, 1.158.6; 7.63.4.
12. *Ibid*, 1.38.2; 230.2; 3.53.5; 61.3; 6.32.5; 7-18.9, 63.4; 10.51Z.4, 73.5; 143.1.
13. *Ibid*, 4.13.3; 10.27.20.
14. *Ibid*, 1.10.2; 105.2.
15. *Ibid*, 1.130.5; 144.3, 158.6.
16. *Ibid*, 3.11.3, 8.69.17.
17. Sinha, A.K., *Reading in Early Indian Socio-Cultural History*, p.50; Verma, Jaya, *op. cit.*, p.137.
18. All these terms are used in the *Ṛgveda* but they did not used in the strict sense. *Varṇa* was used to differentiate between fair skinned and dark skinned; *artha* as we have shown, used in a variety of senses, *kāma* in the same way was used in many usages. So in the *Ṛgveda* these notions are just the 'words' that Rgvedic people used to express their thoughts. They are not used in somewhat technical sense.
19. Pande, G.C., *Foundations of Indian Culture*, Vol.-II, p.70, Sharma, R.S., *Aspects of Political Ideas and Institution in Ancient India*, p.264.
20. Chattopadhyay, K., *Studies in Vedic and Indo-Iranian Religion and Culture*, Vol.-I, Varanasi, 1976, p.115.
21. For details of these notions, see, Hiriyana, M., *Outlines of Indian Philosophy*, p.31; Zimmerman R. "The Evidences of RK-text for the meaning of Rta" in *Proceedings of All India Oriental Conference*, 5th session, Vol-1, Lahore, 1930, pp.214&217; Hindrey, Roderick, *Comparative Ethics in Hindu and Buddhist Traditions*, Delhi, 1978, p.50; Organ, T.W., *The Hindu Quest for the Perfection of Man*, Athens, 1970, p.211; Bloom field, M., *Religion of the Veda*, Delhi 1972, p.26;

Mazumdar, R.C., (ed.) *The Vedic Age*, Bombay 1971, p.369.

22. Gopal, Lallanji, *Pracina Bhartiya Rajnaitik Vicardhara*, p.5
23. *Ṛgveda*, 10.90.12; *Taittiriya Saṁhita*, V.7.6.3-4.
24. Kane, P.V., *op. cit.*, p.111; Pande, G.C., *Foundations of Indian Culture*, Vol. 2, pp.181-182; Mac Donald, K.S., *The Brahmanas of the Vedas*, Delhi, 1979, p.103.
25. Sharma, R.S., *Aspects of Political Ideas and Institutions in Ancient India*, Delhi, 1968, p.263.
26. Titles such as *Adhirāja*, *Virāta*, *Samrāta*, *Ekrāt*, *Svarāj*, *Prajāpati*, *Viswapati* are frequently used in this period for denoting king or his power.
27. In the *Atharvaveda*, *Vājsani Saṁihitā*, *Aitereya Brāhmaṇ*, *Sathpath Brāhmaṇ*, etc. various titles are used for denoting king and his power. The word *ekrāt* was used in the *Ṛgveda* (10.128.9) as well as in the *Atharvaveda* (3.4.1). The word *samrata* was also used in the *Ṛgveda* as well as in *Atharvaveda*. See *Ṛgveda*, I. 25-10; II. 28-6; V 85.1; VI-68.9; VIII. 42.1; *Atharvaveda*, VI. 36.3.
28. Pant, A.D., *A Critical Study of Arthaśāstra Tradition in Ancient Indian Political Thought* (unpublished, D.Litt. Thesis), Allahabad, 1966, p.17.
29. In the *Ṛgveda*, we find references of Assemblies like *sabhā* and *samiti*, *vidatha*, etc. which helped the ruler in solving state-affairs. See, Sharma, R.S., *op. cit.*, pp.270-71.
30. *Maitrāyiṇi Saṁhitā*, II. 6.5; IV 3.8; *Śatapath Brāhmaṇ*, V.3.2; V.4.4.7; *Taittiriya Brāhmaṇ*, I. 8.9.1; Sharma, R.S., *op. cit.*, p.139; Roy, B.P., *Later Vedic Economy*, p.139; Gopal, Lallanji, *op. cit.*, p.53.
31. Roy, B.P., *op. cit.*, p.2.
32. *Vājsaini Saṁhita*, 11.58; *Aitereya Brāhmaṇ*, 8.5; Roy, Jaimal, *The Rural and Urban Economy and Social Change in Ancient India*, p.25.
33. *Atharvaveda*, *Pṛthvi Sūkta*, XII. 1.6, 43,44,45; Sharma, R.S., *op. cit.*, p.274.
34. It is said in the *Satapath Brāhmaṇ*. "...And thus what ever exists here on the earth all that is admitted to sacrifice..." III.6.2.26; Basu, J., *op. cit.*, p.139; Dandekar, R.N., *Insight into Hinduism*, Poona, 1979, Delhi, p.22; Mukherjee, Radha

Kumud, *Hindu Civilization*, Delhi, 1975, p.132-33; Basham, A.L., *op. cit.*, p.34.

35. Gokhale, B.G., *Ancient India-History and Culture*, Bombay 1970, p.151.
36. Kane, P.V., *History of Dharamsastra*, part-I (Hindi Tr.) Lucknow, 1980, p.111.
37. Altekar, A.S., *State and Government in Ancient India*,Delhi, 1984, p. 5.
38. Altekar, A.S., *op. cit.*, p.5.
39. Radha, Krishnan, S., *Indian Philosophy*, part I., p.12.
40. Pande, G.C., *Foundations of Indian Culture*, part-II, p.65.
41. Dutta, D & Chatterji, S., *An introduction to Indian Philosophy*, pp. 64-66; Pandc, G.C., *Mulya Mimamsa*, p.101.
42. Pande, G.C., *Foundation of Indian Culture*, part-II, p.152; *Manusmṛti*, 1.107.
43. *Manusmṛti*, 1.107; Gupta, S.N. *op. cit.*, p.33.
44. *Sankhya karika*, as quoted by Gupta Shantinath, p.168, fn. 11.
45. Pande, G.C., *op. cit.*, p.65.
46. Literally means, the use and employment of rods. See, Kangle, R.P., *The Kauṭilya Arthaśāstra*, A study, part III, p.3; Altekar, A.S., *op. cit.*, p.1; Bhandarkar, D.R., *Some Aspects of Ancient Hindu Polity*, Patna, 1988, p.17
47. Pande, G.C. *op. cit.*, p.153.
48. *Niti* literally means proper guidance, therefore, the one meaning of term is that it was the science of Ethics. Proper guidance or direction usually presupposes propriety, prudence, and wisdom So *Nitiśāstra* also came to denote the science of wisdom and right course. Kamandaka, Bhartrhari, Sukra prefers to name their treatises *Nitiśāstra* rather that *arthaśāstra*, see, Altekar, A.S., *op. cit.*, p.2-3.
49. For details of these terms, see, Kane, P.V., *op. cit.*, Pt.-III, pp.4-8; Altekar, A.S., *op. cit.*, pp.1-4; Kangle, R.P., *op. cit.*, pp.3-5.
50. *Viṣnu Purāna*, III 6.28; *Vāyu Purāṇa*, 61.79; *Brahmaṇda Purāṇa*, 35.88.89.
52. *Mahābhārata*, *Śāntiparva*, 59.14.
53. Ibid, 59.15-20.

54. Ibid, 59-22-24-27.
55. Ibid, 59.35.
56. Ibid, 59-28-29, cf, *Manusmṛti*, 7.14.
57. *Mahābhārata*, Śāntiparva, 59-86-87.
58. Ibid 86-92
59. Ibid 3.58.1.3.
60. Kangle, R.P., *op. cit.*, pp.40 If.
61. Gopal, Lallanji, *op. cit.*, pp.2-3.
62. Ibid, p.3.
63. *Ṛgveda* 10.87-5-8, 10.
64. *Ṛgveda* 10.69. 10.
65. Altekar, A.S., *op. cit.*, p.4.
66. Drekmeier, Charles, *Kingship and Community in Early India*, California, 1987, p.29.
67. Bhandarkar, D.R., *op. cit.*, p.61.
68. Pant, A.D. *Introduction to Beni Prasad's The theory of Government in Ancient India*, Allahabad, 1974, p.17.
69. *Chāndogya Upaniṣad*, VII. 1-2, 1.4.21.
70. For, *Itihāsa-Purāna* occurs in the *Atharvaveda* and only *Itihāsa* in the *Satpath Brāhman* in one place and in compound at other places. *Atharvaveda*, 15.6.4, Satpath Brāhmaṇ singly in 4.3.12.13, and as compound in XI. 5.6.8; 79; *Sarpavidyā* is mentioned also in Satpath *Brāhmaṇ*-13.4.3.9.
71. As Nārada was regarded as his expounder and Narada called himself a mantravi in *Chāndogya Upaniṣad*, therefore, *kstravidya* also falls in the category of Mantra, worldly knowledge. *Chāndogya Upaniṣad*, VII-2; Pant, A.D., *op. cit.*, p.18
72. In the *Upaniṣads* we found the reference of the nature of *Ātma-vidyā*, see, *Muṇdaka Upaniṣad* I. 1-4-5; *Maitrāyaṇi Upaniṣad*, VI. 21.
73. Agarwala, V.S., *India as Known to Panini*, Lucknow, 1953, p. 337.
74. Patanjali, *Mahābhāṣya* IV 260, p.284 (Keilhorṇs ed.)
75. Keith, A.B., Vedic Index, *Kstra-vidyā*.
76. Hopkins, E.W., J.A.OS., XIII, p.104; as quoted by A.D. Pant in his '*Introduction*' *to The Theory of Government in Ancient India of* Beniprasad.

77. Agarwala, V.S., *op. cit.*, p.304.
78. Law, B.C., *India as Known to the Early Texts of Buddhism and Jainism*, pp.258-259.
79. Pant, A.D., *op. cit.*, p.19.
80. *Ibid*, p.20.
81. Rhy David's, *Dialogue of Buddha*, vol. I, p.18.
82. Pant, A.D., *op. cit.*, p.19.
83. *Milinda Pañho*, ed. V. Trenckner, p.164 as quoted by Pant A.D., *op. cit.*, p.20.
84. *Ibid*, p.175.
85. *Vālmiki Rāmāyaṇa*, II. 21.49.
86. *Ibid*, II 104.20.
87. *Mahābhārata*, XII. 136.39.
88. *Māhabhārata*, XII. 136.40.
89. Ghosal, U.N., *History of Indian Political Ideas*, London, 1929, p.66.
90. Barua, B.M., *A History of Pre-Buddhist Indian Philosophy*, Calcutta, 1921, pp.292-93.
91. Mehta, R.L., *Pre-Buddhist India*, Bombay, 1939. p.334.
92. Mukherjee, Radha Kumud, *Ancient Indian Education*, London, 1951.
93. Ghosal, U.N., *op. cit.*, p.66.
94. Pant, A.D., *A Critical Study of the Arthaśāstra Tradition*, p.11.
95. In the *Śāntiprava* of the *Māhābhārata* the duties of king and matters of polity has been dealt as *Rājdharma*.
96. As we have shown Pant is of the view that the science of polity was earlier called *kṣtravidyā*.
97. Kamandaka used the word *Rājavidyā* in the sense of science of polity and statecraft. *Nitisāra*. I. 7-9.
99. Kosambi, Jacobi, Kangle gives the details of these schools as well as individual teachers. On the basis of availabe sources in can be safely concluded that all of these contibuted to the growth of the science of polity.
100. The Manuscript of the *Arthaśāstra* was handed over by a Pandit of Tanjore district to the Mysore Government Oriental Library in 1905 and R. Shamasastry was the first person who immediately used its material in his paper entitled '*Chanakya's* '*Land and Revenue Policy*' in the Indian Antiquary in 1905. On

the basis of *Viṣṇu Purāṇa*, *Nandisūtra*, he assumed that Cāṇakya was the minister of Candragupta in the fourth century B.C. To support his view that *Arthaśāstra* was a production of Mauryan Age he referred to the *Dasakumara Carita* of Dandin, the *Nitisara* of Kamandaka, *Nandisutra*, *Pancatantra* and *Nitivakyamrta* of Soma Deva. See Shama Sastry, R., "Chanakya's land and Revenue policy." *Indian Antiquary*, Bombay, 1905, Vol. XXXI, pp.5-6.

He edited and published the text of the *Arthaśāstra* for the first time in 1909. In 1915 in his preface to the translated text he discussed the genuineness and antiquity of the text and maintained his earlier view. See, Shama Sastry's Preface to his edition of *Arthaśāstra*.

101. Ganapati Sastri also expressed the same view in introduction to his edition of the *Arthaśāstra*.
102. According to Law "the text throws a flood of light on the material, social and political condition of the ancient Hindus during the third and fourth centuries before the Christian era. It is the record of the age of Candragupta." Law, N.N., *Studies in Ancient Hindu Polity* (Indian reprint), Delhi, 1975, p.1. Also, see *The Kauṭilya Arthaśāstra*, in Calcutta Review, XIII, pp.228-38.
103. Smith is of the view that the substance of the precepts and regulations has an extremely archaic aspect, and the polity described is mainly that of the Mauryan age. See, Smith, V.A., *The Early History of India*, (Second edition) Oxford, 1908, p.134.
104. Fleet assigned the text a date between 321 and 296 B.C. and held Kauṭilya to be the author of the text. See, Fleet, J.F., in Preface to Ganapati Sastri's edition of the *Arthaśāstra*.
105. Jayaswal in the Appendix C of his *Hindu Polity* supported the traditional view. See, Jayaswal, K.P., *Hindu Polity*, Appendix-C, Banglore, 1946 pp.368-396.
106. Meyer in his German translation of *Arthaśāstra* supported the traditional view and devoted thirty six pages to indicate the Indian Tradition–Sarkar, B.K., "German Translation of Kautalyan Arthaśāstra." *Indian Historical Quarterly*, 1928, IV., p.375.
107. Bandopadhyaya, N.C., *Development of Hindu polity and*

Political Theories, (reprint) Delhi, 1980, p.76.

108. In the introduction to Law's *Studies in Ancient Hindu Polity*, Mookerji said that the *Arthaśāstra* was the work of Cāṇakya, the minister of Candragupta and therefore belonged to the 4th century B.C. further he writes. "the work was the production of an individual author and not of a school." See, Law, N.N., *Studies in Ancient Hindu Polity*, (introductory Essay) p.X.
109. Thomas was uncertain about the precise date of the *Arthaśāstra* and assumed that the work fall within or near the Mauryan period and used it for an understanding of the period. See, Thomas, F.W., *The Cambridge History of India*, (ed.) E.J. Rapson, Vol. I, Delhi, 1955, pp.467-74.
110. Bhandarkar, D.R., *Some Aspects of Ancient Hindu Polity*, (2nd edition) Varanasi, 1963, pp.49-50.
111. Dikshitar, V.R.R., *The Mauryan Polity*, Madras, 1932, Preface.
112. Kane, P.V., *The History of Dharamsastra*, Vol.-I, Part I, Poona, 1962, pp.197 and onwards.
113. Basak, R.G., in Introduction to his Bengali translation of the *Arthaśāstra*, Vol.-I., Calcutta, 1950.
114. Kosambi, D.D., *An Introduction to the Study of Indian History*, Bombay, 1956, p.199.
115. Breloer, stated that the *Arthaśāstra* was a document of administrative law, the outline of Magnacarta, if not the legislative work of Kaiser Candragupta, which would raise the emperor even above the Roman "Kaiser Justinian"–See, Breloer, B., *Kautaliya-Studien*, Vol. III., leipzing, 1984, p.11. as quoted by Misra, S.C., *Evolution of Kauṭilya's Arthaśāstra*, p.28.
116. Nilakanta Sastri, K.A., *Age of the Nandas and the Mauryas*, Banaras, 1952. pp.190-211.
117. "We may, therefore conclude that there is no convincing reason why this work should not be regarded as the work of Kautilya, who helped Candragupta to come to power in Magadha."- Kangle, R.P., *The Kauṭilya Arthaśāstra -A study, Part-III*, (Reprint) 1988, Bombay, p.106.
118. Kauṭilya's *Arthaśāstra*, 1.1.19.
119. K.A., 5.1.78;
120. Nitisara, 1.4-6.
121. *Daśakumāra Carita*, VIII.

122. (ed.) Majumdar, R.C., *History and Culture of Indian People, Vol. II, The Age of Imperial Unity*, (5th ed.) Bombay, 1980, p.274.
123. *Ibid*, p.274.
124. J. Jolly was the principal among those who opposed the traditional view, though "at first was not against authenticity and antiquity of text." After 1912 he changed his opinion and "held that could be dated in the 3rd Century. A.D.," Jolly. J. and Schmidt, *Arthaśāstra of Kauṭilya, Vol.-I*, Lahore, 1923. p.1, as quoted by Misra, S.C., *op. cit.*, p.20.

124A. Hillebrandt held that "it cannot be assumed that Kauṭilya himself is the sole author of the text in question. It only originated in Kauṭilya's school, for it frequently quotes the opinions of other teachers and contradicts them in the sūtra style by quoting the view of Kauṭilya himself, many times expressing the view of the latter in the form of direct maxims." Hillebrandit, A., as quoted by Kangle, R.P., *op. cit.*, p.101.

125. Winternitz was of view that "it was a creation of an individual and not of the minister of Candragupta." -See, Misra, S.C., *op. cit.*, p.24.
126. Keith, A.B., *A History of Sanskrit Literature*, (Reprint) Oxford, 1956, p.461.
127. "On the strength of an intensive comparison between the Indica of Megasthenes, and the *Arthaśāstra*, it is not possible to discover an agreement as some investigators have stressed and the authorship of Chandragupta's minister for the *Arthaśāstra* doubtful."–Stein, Otto, Megasthenes and Kauṭilya, Vienna, 1922, p.302.
128. For the view of Kalidas Nag, See Misra, S.C., *op. cit.*, p.24.
129. Nath, Pran, "The Date of the Compilation of Kauṭilya's Arthaśāstra", *Indian Antiquary*, 1931, Vol. LX. pp. 112-121.
130. Raychaudhri, H.C., *History and Culture of Indian People*, Vol. II, pp.285-86.
131. Bose, A.N., "The date of the Arthaśāstra of Kauṭilya," in *Indian Culture*, vol. IV, p.435.
132. Misra, S.C., *op. cit.*, p.39-40.
133. Johnston, E.H., "Two studies in the Arthaśāstra of Kauṭilya", *Journal of the Royal Asiatic Society of Great Britain and Ireland*, 1929, pp.77-86.

134. Bhandakar in his *Presidential address* to the first oriental conference, Poona, "favoured for Kauṭilya a date between the first and the second century A.D." -Mishra, S.C., *op. cit.*, p. 23.
135. Raychaudhri, H.C., *op. cit.*, p. 286.
136. Basham, A.L., *The Wonder that was India*, London, 1966, p.77.
137. *Arthaśāstra*, 15.1.
138. Keeping in view this importance of inhabited land, Kauṭilya included *janapada* in the seven constituents of the state. See, *Arthaśāstra.*, 6.1; also *Manu Smrti*. 9.294.
139. Kangle, R.P., *The Kauṭilya Arthaśāstra*, Part-I-II, III. Bombay.
140. Pande, G.C., *Foundations of Indian Culture*, part-II, p.153
141. *Kāmasūtra*, 1.5-8.
142. *Nitiprakasika*, 1.21.22.
143. *Buddhacarita*, 1.46.
144. Kane, P.V., *History of Dharmasastra*, Vol.-II, p. 580.
145. cf. Yadava, B.N.S., *Presidential Address*, Ancient Indian section, Proceedings of Indian History Congress, Bombay, 1980, p. 23.
146. Pande, G.C., *op. cit.*, p.153.
147. Ibid.
148. Commarswami, A.K., *Spiritual Authority and the Temporal Power in the Indian Theory of Government*, Delhi, p. 2.
149. *Śatpath Brāhmaṇ*, 5.4.4.7.
150. *Gautam Dharamsutra*, 11.9.10; *Vasistha Dharamsutra*, 21.7.9; *Baudhayana Dharamasutra*, 1.10.18.
151. Pande, G.C., *op. cit.*, p.153.
152. Ibid.
153. *Mahābhārata*, *Śāntiparva*, 56.101, 102; Pande. G.C., *op. cit.*, p.154-55.
154. *Arthaśāstra*, 1.2.5.
155. *Nitisāra*, 1.21.60, VIII-1.
156. Pande. G.C., *op. cit.*, p.159.
157. Ibid.
158. *Śukra Nitisāra*. 1-2-4, 4.3.56., 3.176, 3.177, 1.78-79.

4. *Arthaśāstra* and the *Purūśārtha*

Man, primarily, is a value-seeking being. This value seeking, inherent in his natural instinct, differentiates him from other living beings and assigns him a higher place among them.[1] Along with this value-seeking nature man is also a socio-cultural being and his choice of values certainly emerges from that socio-cultural atmosphere in which he lives and grows.[2] Thus, cultural heritage put great influence on the choice of values. Every civilization owns its distinct cultural heritage and this heritage plays an important role in the reconstruction of the mental-make-up of the people who belongs to it.[3] Owing to this peculiarity, the conception of values, and the nature of *summum bonum* vary in different civilizations. In the ancient Greek civilization, emphasis was laid on the socio-political aspect of human life, and the formation of society or state was thought to be the *summum bonum*.[4] On the other hand, in ancient Indian civilization man had been considered as to be a moral-spiritual being and his highest goal was a to attain salvation through transcending this world of will and desires.[5] So the ethos of Indian culture is primarily spiritual. Along with this spiritualistic outlook of life ancient Indian tradition gave due importance to the material and empirical necessities of life which were manifested through the ideals of *Pṛavati*.[6] In ancient India two lines of thoughts prevailed simultaneously, *Karmamārga* and *Jñānamārga*. *Karmamārga* was manifested through *pravati* and received its culmination in Vedic ideals of *yajña*, and *svarga*. *Jñānamārga* was manifested through the idea of *nivṛtti* in the *Upaniṣads* when the division of *śreya-preya* was made and to attain *mokṣa* became the highest ideal. Chiefly the followers of heterodox sects developed the idea of *nivrtti*. (i.e. Jain, Buddhist).[7] An attempt of coordinating of both these thoughts was made in the *epics* though, *Upaniṣads* also made preliminary attempts. This idea of synthesis of two opposite poles received maturity in the epics and as a result of it the notion of *Purūṣārtha-Catuṣṭay* was developed. This does not imply that the values included in this scheme were not prevailed in country earlier. No doubt idea of *trivarga* (*dharma*, *artha*, *kāma*) was prevailed and its roots could be traced up to Ṛgvedic age. The notion of *mokṣa* was also developed in the later Vedic age but the synthesis of these values in the form of *Caturvarga* theory was done at the later date. So the notion of *purūṣārtha* could be regarded as the scheme of values in Indian tradition, thus, could be taken as the representative of Indian value system. After developing an acquaintance with the notion of *artha* and *arthaśāstra* in the historical perspective, it will be now appropriate to discuss the notion of *Purūṣārtha*.

The word *purūṣārtha* is a synthesis of two words, *pūruṣa* and *artha*. The word *purūṣa* is derived from *pu*-meaning *pur* (house) body. *Puri sete iti purusa*. i.e. the conscious being that sleeps, dwells, resides, in the body is *purūṣa*.[8] The compound meaning of word *purūṣa*, according to this derivation, is 'the being' only.[9] But as shown in *Bhāgvata Purāṇa*, the word, *purūṣa* is used in Indian thoughts chiefly for human being not only for being.[10] So the word *purūṣa* in term of *purūṣārtha* signifies human person-man or woman.[11] *Artha-Arthayate Prāthayate sarveh iti artha*. According to this derivation 'the object of desire is *artha*'. So the literally meaning of the word *purūṣārtha* is "the object desired by a *purūṣa*."[12] Thus, whatever man desires, whatever is his chief goal, the pleasure and comfort which he wishes, and whatever is the most desirable for him, for achieving which, he makes continuous efforts is *purūṣārtha*.[13] The word *purūṣārtha* in totality includes all those things and objects of pursuits that a man can desire for fulfilling his wishes. The foremost wish of every individual is the survival of his life because it was only after survival that a man can think about other objectives of life. This wish is included in *purūṣārtha* in the form of *artha*, which being a material value is essential for the survival of a man. Along with it three other aspirations, closely related to the human life is included in this scheme. The Indian value-system thus, recognized four objectives of human life. The *Agni pūraṇa* states that *dharma*, *artha*, *kāma* and *mokṣa* are the four *purūṣārtha*.[14] Indian tradition unanimously agreed that all aims and aspirations of human person could be comprised in these four words and categories.[15] The most significant characteristic of the Indian value-system, manifested through the theoretical conception of *purūṣārtha* is the co-ordination between material and spiritual values.[16] As the notion of *purūṣa* in itself includes all level of consciousness from biological to spiritual. So the Indian seers combined together the achievements of human person, from biological to spiritual, in a synthesize form in the notion of *purūṣārtha*.[17] The values included in this scheme of *purūṣārtha* can be classified into two broad categories, namely instrumental values and absolute values. While *kāma* and *mokṣa* can be termed as absolute values, *artha* and *dharma* can be regarded as instrumental values. *Artha* is the instrument of achieving *kama* and *dharma* is the instrument of achieving *moksa*. These values are also classified as *trivarga* and *caturvarga*. The first three temporal values viz, *dharma*, *artha*, *kama* are called *trivarga*[18] because they helped man in achieving worldly goals. *Dharma* in this scheme of *trivarga* is a regulatory values and the fourth value *mokṣa* is transcendental in nature, therefore, presents the highest level of human desires, transforming *trivarga* into *caturvarga*. Whatever the classification may be made, there may be no second opinion to this conclusion that all these values are the values of life and includes in their sphere all those aims and objectives that a human person desires, thus, are meaningful for all, for them also who wishes to achieve material and empirical goals and for them also whose aim is to attain spiritual upliftment. *Arthaśāstra* is the science of *artha* and *artha*, as we have already indicated, initially stands for value. With the development of the notion of *purūṣārtha*, the idea of *artha* has also been included in it and as a part of it *artha* denoted politico-economic value. In this connotation it included in its sphere all the material possessions, comforts, matters of polity, statecraft, economic welfare and security. These are the basic necessities of life and without them human existence is impossible. All these necessities can be had only in a peaceful atmosphere. So *artha* in this scheme is a politico-economic value. *Artha*, therefore, is the foundation upon which the whole structure of life has been built. Being a part of this four-fold value scheme, it possesses a close relationship with the other values of this scheme. In this chapter the relationship that *artha* have with the other values of this scheme will be discussed through developing and acquaintance with the notion of *dharma*, *kama* and *mokṣa* in historical perspective. All of these values have their own conception in Indian culture and none of them can be neglected if a balanced life is to be pursued.

Notion of *Dharma*

Dharma is a unique concept in ancient Indian value-system. Its connotation is very wide and to define it in concrete terms is not an easy task.[19] In its various meanings, *dharma* stands for ordinance, usage, duty, right, justice, virtue, religion, good works, functions, or characteristics.[20] *Dharma* as Zimmer said, "refers not only to the whole context of law and custom (religion, usage, ethics, good works, virtue, religious or moral merit, justice, piety impartiality) but also to the essential nature, character, or quality of the individual as a result of which his duty, social function, vocation or moral standard is what it is."[21] Thus, to define *dharma* in exact term is not easy but a general thing that can be found in all forms of *dharma* is its abstract co-ordination with just, right and good. Whatever is just, right and good is *dharma* and the opposite is *adharma*.[22]

It is said in the *Taittirīya Āraṇayaka*[23] that *dharma* is the foundation of the whole universe. In this world people go unto a person who is best vested in *dharma* for guidance. By means of *dharma* one drives away evil. Upon *dharma* everything is founded. Therefore, *dharma* is called the highest good. The *Mahābhārata* clearly accepts that for the sake of the promotion of strength and efficacy among beings the declaration of *dharma* is made.[24]

The term *dharma* derived from the root *dhr*, (to support, to uphold, to nourish, to sustain)[25] means that "which sustains one's life and therefore, implies the conviction or faith which holds as it were one's entire existence."[26] While defining *dharma* it is said in the *Māhabhārata* that which maintains, regulates holds a things is *dharma*. So whatever everything that have upholding, sustenance is *dharma*.[27] The concept of *dharma*, thus, comprised precepts that aim at securing the material and spiritual sustenance and growth of the individual society.[28] '*Dhāraṇaparakatā*' or sustenance is the natural characteristic of *dharma* and the conception of *dharma* can be understood on the basis of this characteristic.[29]

This *dhāraṇaparakatā* (i.e. the upholding power of

dharma) is the essential element of any existence either at any level in universe or on the earth.[30] Sustenance possesses direct relation with the order, thus, *dharma* is that which maintains order.[31] *Ṛta* stands for an order or system, in the Vedic literature and the same order or system is manifested by *dharma* on this earth of human beings through "developing a multidimensional code of conduct applicable into each and every sphere of human life in all ages and stages".[32] *Dharma* is a dynamic notion and in practical world it comes forward in the form of a system that should to be maintained at every cost if peace and harmony are to be established in a society. *Dharma* in its essence is an ethical or moral consciousness inherent in human nature distinguishing him in the world of animals[33] that forms "the threads of interaction and interrelation between the individuals, thus this paved the way for the development of a society".[34]

A glance over the historical development of Indian culture would show that *dharma* possesses a close relation with the *ṛta*[35] (the moral cosmic order of Ṛgvedic age). Though in the *Ṛgveda* the word '*dharma*' and '*dharman*' are referred to many times[36] but achieves meaningfulness only with reference to *ṛta*.[37] *Dharma*, as said earlier, is the earthly manifestation of *ṛta*.[38] In the *Ṛgveda*, *ṛta* is conceptualized as a fundamental order that controls whole cosmos.[39] It regulates everything in the creation either static or moving.[40] It is unalterable, distance and time can make no alteration in it.[41] Seasons change due to it.[42] Due to *ṛta* sun rises and sets daily. *Ṛta* is prior to creation. Gods are created from *ṛta* (*ṛta-jāta*). Due to *Ṛta* they performs their relative duties.[43] According to *Ṛgveda Mitra-Varuṇa* has possessed a close relation with *ṛta*.[44] *Varuṇa* has been depicted as the guardian of *ṛta*.[45] But they also get power from *ṛta*[46] and through *ṛta* they rule over the world.[47]

Ṛta worked through its three dimensional form.[48] In its

first dimension *ṛta* worked on natural level controls the order of creation. Rise and set of sun, moon, change of seasons, all works of nature goes on under the regulation of *ṛta*. In its second form *ṛta* comes us on ritual or sacrificial level.[49] *Yajñas*, in the Vedic literature, had been regarded as the root of creation, thus, *yajña*-rituals where also a form of creation.[50] As *ṛta* regulated process of creation, therefore, the rules and regulations through which *yajñas* were regulated also thought to be a manifestation[51] of *ṛta*. In its third form *rta* works as a moral regulation between human beings. The same order works between the human beings that work between different celestial bodies. So the second and the third dimension of *ṛta* are connected directly with the worldly affairs. In human life it is expressed through the concept of *dharma* and *satya*, through the ideas of sustenance, maintenance, upholding in the former and that of existence, in the latter.[52] In human relations *ṛta* works as *satya*. It is the summary of the human life and behaviour. According to *Ṛgveda*, *ṛta* and *satya* all originated together.[53] *Satya* is the manifestation of *ṛta*.[54]

The concepts of *dharma* and *satya* are related intimately and are inseparable. In fact they are one and the same rooted jointly in *ṛta* and making the human world existent. It is the upholding of *dharma* that makes things *satya* by establishing them existent. (*satta*)

It is quite clear from the foregoing account that both *ṛta* and *dharma* are the two sides of the same coin. Later on the conception of *ṛta* continues its journey in the form of *dharma*. The scope of *ṛta* was restricted to the affairs of creation and nature. In human life it was substituted by *dharma* that merges all the elements of sustenance (*dhāraṇparakatā*) in its notion, thus, achieves the special and unique significance. On the one hand *dharma* as the ritual manifestation of *ṛta* codifies the rules and regulations of sacrifices,[55] this presents itself as the substitute of *ṛta* and on the other hand for the existence (*satta*) of human life and world adopts the shapes of regulator of human conduct.

In the *Taittirīya Upaniṣad*[56] and *Bṛhadāraṇayaka Upaniṣad*[57] *satya* has been taken equivalent to *dharma* and it is said that one should move towards *satya* from *asatya*. In reference to human life '*satya*' is the first and foremost *dharma* that upholds human life and society and due to its natural characteristic of *dhāraṇparakatā*, it upholds many other virtues that are essential for moral upliftment of human being.[58] Indian culture evolves the integrated and multidimensional concept of *dharma* for the full-fledged development of the human being. *Dharma*, on the one hand, in the form of general code (*sāmānya dharma*)[59] includes the methods, rules, elements that are essential for the development of one's personality irrespective of social status, age, class, caste any another difference, then on the other hand in the form of specified duties, (*viśiṣta dharma*), divided into categories like, *Varṇadharma*, *Kuladharma*, *Āśramadharma*, *Deśhdharma*, *Jātidharma*, *Srenidharma*,[60] builds a series of duties and obligations[61] for a man according to his position in society, space, and country. *Samanya dharma* and *visista dharma* are complementary to each other. The former is the primary condition for the latter because it transforms the biological human being into cultured man and man through developing his tendencies, capacities, instincts, constructs society.[62] *Dharma* is that principles through which we pass our lives and our social relations are established. It is the truth of the life and the power to deternine our nature.[63]

In historical perspective the concept of *dharma* existed from the age of *Ṛgveda* and its tradition developed in the later period. Dharamaśāstra deals with it and develops a code of conduct applicable in all spheres of lifc. *Sāmānya dharma* consists of virtues that are essential for the moral development of man like, mercy, kindness, forgiveness, etc.

These virtues, though prevailed in Vedic age,[64] but raised to prominence in Upaniṣadic age.[65] In the Epic age, the realm of these virtues exceed. In the *Mahābhārata* the number of these virtues increased and their mutual dependence was established in such a manner that if one *dharma* was performed fully in the right way, then other would be performed automatically. Describing the importance of the truth in the list of general code (*sāmānya dharma*)[66] *Śāntiparva* says, truh is the universal *dharma*. It is the highest *yajña* and everything depends on it.[67] While Patanjali described five virtues, Manu numerates ten virtues.[68] Yājñavalkya described nine virtues.[69] In fact with the need and situation the number of virtues included in this *dharma* increased. There is reference of thirty virtues in the Purāṇas.[70] Virtues included in the General code (*sāmānya dharma*) aim to develop the moral consciousness of man and through this moral upliftment help in the attainment of *mokṣa*. *Viśiṣta dharma* (specified code) is basically the social duties relative to one's position in the society. They include *varṇadharma*, *āsramadharma*, *kuldharma*, *jatidharma*, etc.

Therefore, both these codes of conduct are essential for man and it is expected from him in the *Dharamśastras* that he will never give up the path of *dharma* in any situation. So the *dharma*, for Indians is a multi dimensional concept that existed from an early period and developed in a specific way in the later centuries. In the Indian way of life clear dominance of *dharma* can be witnessed in every sphere of life. *Dharamśāstra* writers hold that *dharma* is the most important value in the *trivarga*. Āpastamba Dharmasūtra declares that a man should enjoy all such pleasures as are not opposed to *dharma*. In this way one secures both worlds.[71]

Dharma, in Indian tradition, is the principle by which *artha* and *kāma* are kept within bounds. It prevents the person from deciding either *artha* or *kāma* or any combination of *artha* and *kāma* as the sole end of life. It is the valuational check which brings restrain upon the pursuits of wealth and pleasure reminding the pursuer that while these belong to the life of man they are not ends in themselves. According to the *Mahābhārata*, "A wise man tries to secure all three but if three cannot be attained he secures *dharma* and *artha* or *dharma* if he has a choice of only one from among the three"[72] *Dharma* is the source of both *artha* and *kāma*.[73] Yājñavalkya said that one should consider *dharma* to be most important. It is also said in *Yājñavalkyasmrti*, "*dharma* is the source of *artha* but not vice versa; for *dharma* can be performed without the help of *artha*, but without *dharma*, there will be no bit of *artha*."[74]

But this is the point of view of *Dharamaśāstra* writers. Kauṭilya on the other hand, as a writer of *Arthaśāstra* gives prime importance to *artha*. According to him both *dharma* and *kama* are rooted in *artha*.[75] Vātsyāyana presents a different idea. *Kāmasutra* places *dharma* first for ordinary people, but *artha* first for kings and *kāma* first for public women.[176] Thus, *artha* and *dharma* both are the important principles of life. Among them which is important depends entirely on the nature of the concerned people.

Concept of *Kāma*

The concept of *kāma* stands for the eloquent expression of the deep psychological insights of the Hindu philosophers. In the scheme of *Purūṣārtha-Catuṣṭay* though it is included as the third end of the human life but being related deeply to the primary levels of biological consciousness it is primarily important for the human being. In the *Ṛgveda* it is said to have been the first movement that arose in One[77] and has been mentioned as a great cosmogonic force.[78] It is said in the *Ṛgveda* that longing for happiness and the fulfillment of the desires is *kāma*.[79] Ancient Indian seers realized the importance of mental health and a satisfied life. They were well aware that the good life that is a sure way towards the spiritual attainment is based on the preparation and discipline at the lower levels.[80] Some psychic forces cannot be repressed or negated because it may lead to guilt, remorse, and frustration. Thus, they acknowledged the importance of *kāma* in human life and accepted it as the value of life.

Literally '*kāma*' means desire or wish,[81] but it is a narrow sense because idea of *kāma* is not limited to merely desires but the in wider sense this includes the desire and the pleasure that is received due to fulfillment of desir.[82] Various situations that human mind experienced between desire and its fulfillment are different situations of *kāma*. Pleasure is the culmination of *kāma* and *artha* is the means of it. The sensitiveness of senses and the pleasure achieved through them are the two extremities between which the conception of *kāma* develop. As the achievement of pleasure and pain is the mental experience, in this way, the consciousness of *kāma* is extended from the sensuous level to the mental and therefore transforms the achievement of senses into the mental achievement. "The word *kāma* therefore includes not merely the pleasure of senses but also pleasures derived from the exercise of the mental faculties".[83] According to the *Mahābhārata*, the term *kāma* is used to denote pleasures or happiness derived from contact with external object of senses on the sources of intellectual or emotional satisfaction.[84] Thus all the desired means or objects such as wife, son, house, agricultural land, wealth, eatables, drinks, dance, music, singing, clothes, etc, and the desired objects in the other world are also included in the notion of *kāma*.[85] The mental determination that inspires one to proceed towards pleasure and objects of achieving pleasure is also *kāma* because *kāma* originates due to the determination of mind.[86] The word *kāma*, thus, can be used mainly in following connotations:[87]

1. Pleasure
2. Means of pleasure
3. Desire of pleasure.

According to the *Mahābhārata* that the joy received through the increase of wealth and material possession is also *kāma*. It is regarded as the source of *dharma* and *artha*.[88] It has been taken as the essence of *dharma* and distinguishing among *dharma* and *artha*. Kṛṣṇa in the *Bhagwadgītā* identifies himself with *kāma* that is not opposed to *dharma*.[89] According to the Rāmāyaṇa, the desire of unachieved object is *kama*.[90] Kauṭilya put it in the last category and said one should enjoy *kāma* without detriment to *dharma* and *artha*.[91] Prastapada used *kāma* in a wider sense. He includes in its scope along with worldly desires, the desire of the pleasure and comforts of heaven. Vātsyāyana defines *kāma* as a tendency or disposition which when excited into actions operates at four distinct levels, viz mind, self, senses and the object of sense.[92] *Kāma* thus taken as "to mean pleasure resulting out of sensual, amorous, aesthetic and artistic enjoyment of life". It is an intrinsic value and cannot be ruled out by any higher, moral or spiritual principle. *Kāma*, therefore, is an absolute and intrinsic goal of life which has its distinct but proper place in the total scheme of values.[93]

In the historical perspective the beginning of the idea of material pleasure and aesthetics in ancient India dates back to Harappan age. On the basis of available material artifacts, one can admit unhesitatingly that both these ideas were prevalent in that culture. But what was the exact nature of thinking on this aspect of life can't be said with certainty. This culture was economically very prosperous as the archaeological remains indicate. The great bath, big granary, planned roads, evidences of trade relations with other contemporary civilizations clearly reveals that it was a rich civilization where people preferred to live a life of material comforts. The artifacts found in excavations such as terracotta figurines, copper and bronze images, seals, etc. give the indication of their love for aesthetics. Harappan people were well familiar with the ideas of material comfort and aesthetics gave them a higher place in their lives. In the Vedic period, the earliest reference of the word *kāma* is found in the *Nāsadiya-sūkta* of the *Ṛgveda*[94] where it is said that in the beginning neither there was *sat* nor *asat* then *kāma* was originated. The whole creation was its transmigration. As already indicated a thorough and careful study of the *Ṛgveda* would reveal that the people of those early days had a strong world affirming attitude having no interest in other worldly affairs. They demanded all the means of worldly enjoyments, material comforts and worshipped gods for fulfilling these desires. The ideas of *artha* and *kāma* were prevalent in this age and were the highest objectives of the people of this age. With the development of the notion of *svarga* as a culmination of all material pleasures and comforts, the desires of Aryans were shifted from the earthly to the heavenly plane. This can be taken as an extension of the pleasure-consciousness of early Aryans and in the later saṁhitās one could trace the roots of this consciousness, though theoretical conception was developed at a later date. Still attaining maximum sensuous pleasure was considered to be the ultimate value but it was now idealized in the form of *svarga.*[95] Now their objective was to achieve the '*svarga*' and *yajñas* were the medium through which it could be achieved. When the ritualistic complexities of *yajñas* increased then a reaction was born against them. The *jñanamargi* branch of thought arose that turned *yajñas* into symbolic entity.[96] *Upaniṣads* through making a clear distinction between *preya* and *śreya,*[97] declared that worldly pleasures are transitory and one should try to achieve more higher goals in one's life, thus attainment of *mokṣa* and *brahman* became the highest objective of life. In the period of *Upaniṣads*, thus, we found that spiritualism dominated the scene but the other aspects of life were also not neglected. In the *Bṛhadārayaṇaka Upaniṣad* Yājñavalkya had expressed his wishes for wealth and worldly comforts.[98] It is said in the *Chāndogya Upaniṣad* that when one got pleasure then one does any work. No one works without pleasure. So one should desire pleasure.[99] A kind of psychological hedonism is praised in this thinking. But as the spiritualism was the dominating factor *mokṣa* was regarded as the highest objective, therefore, *kāma*, that signifies worldly pleasures, has given a low ranking. This does not mean that idea of *kāma* was totally neglected; on the other hand in the *Upaniṣads* we find the instances that people tried to attain the highest goal only after fulfilling their worldly duties. Yājñvalkya took saṁyasa after living a satisfied married life with two wives. Videha ruler Janaka, Cakrāyana, Āruni, etc. were the householder philosophers. So it is quite clear that though propounding the objective of *mokṣa* as highest goal, Upaniṣads did not totally discard worldly pleasures and gave due importance to them, terming them as *preya*. Philosophers like Yājñavalkya and Āruni Uddālaka gave importance to *kāma*. The *mantha*-doctrine was propounded by Uddālaka on the basis of the rules of which has been founded the practical application of the principle of Eugenics at later a date.[100] The credit of the origin of the marriage institution was given to Śevataketu by the *Mahābhārata* clearly reveals that *kāma* had been given a high place in the life of people though the philosophy of the Upanisads was spiritual in nature.[101]

The materialistic thoughts were expounded most clearly by the school of Cārāvakas which has been regarded as the only school of materialistic thinking among Indian philosophers. They propounded the doctrine of hedonism.

Cārāvakas held that one should try to achieve pleasure and only pleasure in this life.[102] They discarded the spiritual and moral ideas altogether and gave importance only to values of *artha* and *kāma*. According to them *artha* was the means to attain the highest objective '*kāma*'.[103]

The school of Cārāvakas was divided into two groups. One group was formed by those whom that advocate a life of gross sensual pleasure was called cunning Cārāvaka and the other one was those whom devoted themselves to the pursuit of more refined pleasures. Vātāsyāyan followed this group.[104] They developed a cultured and refined form of headonism.[105] Vatasyayana, though, wrote a detailed treatise on the science of erotics namely '*Kāmasūtra*' but he laid emphasis on living a balanced life through the proper use of *trivarga*.[106]

The idea of *kāma* was also expressed though indirectly, in the philosophy of sāṁakhya[107] that declares *prakrati* evolves the world of objects when it comes into contact with *purūṣa*. The Jain and Buddhist philosophy, though, was treated, as philosophies of *nivṛtti* putting emphasis on renunciation of world and liberation from bondage, but they did not discard the value of *artha* and *kāma* altogether. The Jain philosophers gave due importance to the pleasures of a married life but simultaneously warned against the excess of sexual pleasure. Mahavir included the *brahmacarya* in the list of vows, but these vows were mainly for *bhiksus*. The rules for householders were different. Hemchandra held that a householder should perform *dharma purūṣārtha*, *artha purūṣārthas* and *kāma purūṣārtha*, in balanced manner.[108]

Buddha propounded the middle path for the pursuits of pleasure. Buddha was of the view that performing vows with *brahmarcarya*, is the essence of life. It is one end. There is no harm in performing pleasure pursuits. This is the second end. The *kāma* that is in full consonance with *dharma*, should be pursued.[109] So it is quite clear that Buddha did not discard the value of pleasure in life but advocated a middle path for achieving it.

The Bhagwad Gītā also advocated this path. Kṛṣṇa identifies himself with *kāma* that is not opposed to *dharma*.[110] According to Gītā inspite of following either the path of *pṛavati* or *nivṛtti*, it would be better to follow a mid-way. Therefore, it propounded the idea of *niṣkāma karma* i.e. action with detatchment.[111] Therefore *kāma* has been regarded as an important value in Indian way of life from the earliest period. As Indian tradition did not favour unlimited material pleasure therefore the idea of *kāma* was regulated by *dharma*.

Kāma in the Indian value system has been taken as an end and *artha* has been taken as 'means' that helps in its achievement.[112] As indicated earlier, *kāma* stands for satisfaction and *artha* for desire. Desire is extrinsic value and the fulfillment of the desire gives pleasure and satisfaction. The pleasure and satisfaction, thus, is intrinsic value. Therefore, on temporal level the highest aim of human life is the achievement of *kāma*, following the path of *dharma* and *artha*. *Artha* is important because without it *kāma* cannot be achieved. When there is no desire or material possession to fulfill desire, how satisfaction can achieve? If there is a desire then only satisfaction can have through its fulfillment. So the basic pre-requisite for *kāma* is *artha*. Without *artha*, *kāma* is of no value. But *artha* is also the enjoyment of *kāma*. If it cannot give any satisfaction or pleasure to man then *artha* is of no use. As *kāma* is an end no doubt it is equally important. In fact both are interrelated. Kauṭilya kept *kāma* at third level and said one should enjoy *kāma* provided there should be no conflict with *dharma* and *artha*. One should not lead a life of no pleasures as pleasure is also an important aspect of life.

Idea of *Mokṣa*

Mokṣa is the pivot on which all the systems of Indian philosophy revolve.[113] *Mokṣa* that initially means liberation has been regarded in Indian value tradition as the culmination of human life.[114] and in this form has been given a highest place in the scheme of values. In fact the scheme of *purūṣārtha* is the golden path that helps and equips man to attain the final destiny through maintaining a proper balance between temporal and spiritual attainments of life. The concept of *mokṣa* thus, is the highest culmination of Indian value tradition.[115] *Mokṣa* is the highest value after realizing which nothing remains to be unrealised.[116] Indian value system can be divided into two broad categories. One group constituted by *dharma*, *artha* and *kāma*, is collectively called *trivarga*, along with the value of *mokṣa* these three values of life constitute the another group that is called *Caturvarga*. The distinction between them has been maintained by the difference that exists between empirical and transcendental value. The state of *mokṣa* implies an idea of transcendence from empirical categories. It is, though, expected from the every Indian individual that he will make efforts to attain this *varga* through the proper use of *trivarga* but it is not an easy task and every one can not attain it.[117] It is said in the *Kathopaniṣad* that it is not a bow that everyone can hang it on his shoulders rather, the path of *mokṣa* is as difficult as walking on the edge of knife.[118] Owing to this it has been accorded the highest place among the four *purūṣārthas*.

The word '*mokṣa*' is derived from a root '*muc*'[119] which means to give up, to get rid of, to leave, or be free from. It means liberation, emancipation and freedom. *Mukti* has the same connotation. *Mokṣa* is that stage after attaining which, man gets freedom, liberation from all kinds of bondage. The *Bṛhadāraṇayaka Upaniṣad* refers to *mukti* as a fourfold release ritually affected by the *hotṛ*, *adhvaryu*, *udgāta*, and *brahma* officiating priests.[120] It is further stated that only when all desires lodge in the heart are liberated (*mukti*) then a mortal become immortal and attain *Brahman*.[121] *Mokṣa*, therefore, is the stage of liberation from all kinds of boundage. Boundage, according to Indian philosophers is the process of birth and rebirth due to the continuous flow of *karmas* and the consequent miseries to which an individual is subject[122] and whole philosophy in India is developed to find a way out for liberation from this bondage. Some philosophers hold that main cause of these sorrows is ignorance.[123] According to them, to get rid of this ignorance is *mokṣa*.[124]

In his *Nyāyasūtra*, Gautam says that *mokṣa* is the blessing of the extinction of false and illusive knowledge and obtaining the true knowledge destructive of lust and hate which corrupt the soul.[125] According to *Advaita Vedāntins*, *mokṣa* "is a condition which not merely involves the extinction of all sufferings and unhappiness, but is also a positive state of supreme and unalloyed bliss. It is a result of self realisation."[126] *Mokṣa*, signifies a stage of inseparable unity between *Ātman* and *Brahman*.[127] It is nothing but self-realisation[128] which can be attained along with knowledge, through wisdom.[129]

As the true nature and essence of *Ātman* is eternal bliss and intelligence, thus, it is a stage of unconditional and eternal happiness. After realizing the true nature of *Ātman* nothing left to be known and one attains perfect liberation and happiness.[130] It is, generally, accepted that in the early Vedic period spiritual thinking found no place in the life of Aryans. As the forerunner of other worldly elements, the ideas of *svarga* and *naraka* could be traced here and there. But careful study of *Ṛgveda* revealed that *Asya Vamasya Sukta* could be regarded as the forerunner of the spiritual thinking that later on developed to a great extent. The spiritual ideas in India prevailed in full swing in the period of *Āryaṇakas* and *Upaniṣads*. The sole aim of the *Upaniṣadic* philosophy was to reveal the ultimate reality. All the philosophies that developed in India, except Cārāvaka, accepts *mokṣa* as the highest objective of life and their whole thinking was directed towards the attainment of this end though they used different terms to denote it such as *kaivalya*, *nirvāṇa*, *mokṣa*, *mukti*, etc. In ancient India the idea of *mokṣa* was highly appreciated. It stood for highest goal of life. But this does not mean that all the other values are neglected. Rather, an idea of harmony was prevalent according to which *mokṣa* could be attained only when there was a harmony among the *dharma*, *artha*, *kāma*. Only then the right social order could be evolved and sustained. The *āśarama* system was planned for the achievement of all the goals of *purūṣārtha*. It is said that one should learn about *dharma* in *Brahmacarya* and should use it in whole span of life. In the *Grastha asarama*, man should try to achieve *artha* and *kāma* and during the last two *āśramas*, *Vānaprastha* and *Saṁyas* one should try to attain *mokṣa*.

So the path of *mokṣa* could be achieved only through following the path of *trivarga*. As *artha* stood for material well being in this scheme, thus it is considered as the lowest objective to be pursued by a man. On the other hand, *mokṣa* in the highest values in this scheme, the highest cannot be achieved without achieving the lowest level, thus *artha* helps in the attainment of *moksa*.

NOTES AND REFERENCES

1. *Aitereya Āraṇayaka*, 2.3.2; Hiriyana, M., *Indian Conception of Values*, Mysore, 1975, p.5.
2. Mukherjee, R.K., *The Destiny of Civilization*, Bombay, 1964, pp.31-32.
3. Mukherjee, R.K., *op. cit.*, p.23.

4. Sabine, G.H., *A History of Political Theory*, New York, 1961, p.355.
5. Zimmer, H., *Philosophies of India* (ed.) J.Campbell (reprint), New York 1956, p.4; Dandekar, R.N., 'The Role of Man in Hinduism' in *Religion of the Hindus* (ed.) K.W. Morgan, New York, 1953, p.135. Sinha, A.K., *Pracina Bharatiya Vaiyakitk and Samajik MulyaBodh*, Allahabad, 1981, p.105.
6. Kuhan Raja, C., *The Vedas*, Waltair, 1957, p.286; Pandey, R.B., *op. cit.*, p.52.
7. Pande, G.C., *Baudha Dharam Kei Vikas Ka Itihasa*, Lucknow, 1976, p.3.
8. Bhagwan Das, *Purūṣārtha*, 1966, Varanasi, p.47.
9. Tripathi, P.V., *Purūṣārtha Catustay*, Varanasi, 1970, p.5.
10. *Bhagvata Purana*, 11.7.21.; 3.20.50.; 7.11.22.
11. Tripathi, P.V., *op. cit.*, p.5.
12. Tripathi, P.V., *op. cit.*, p.5; Hiriyana, M., *op. cit.*, pp. 6-7.
13. *Unadi Sutra*, 2-4.
14. *Agni Purana*, धमार्थकाम मोक्ष च पुरुषार्थ उदाहृताः ।
15. *Manu Smrti*, 2.12-1 3 *Padam Purāṇa*, Utarkhand, A.2.48.
16. Pandey, R.B., *Hindu Dharma Kosa*, 1988, p.409; Lal, Kanvar, *The Cult of Desire*, Delhi, 1982, p.19; Devaraj, N.K., *The Mind and Spirit of India*, Varanasi, 1967, p.96; Murty, Satya, K., *Indian Heritage and Culture*, p.75.
17. Hiriyana, M., *op. cit.*, pp.6-7.
18. Creel, Austin, *Dharma in Hindu Ethics*, Calcutta, 1977, p.11.
19. The term *dharma* cannot be taken as an equivalent to English Religion. "*Dharma* is neither religion, nor philosophy, nor culture exclusively, it is all the three rolled into one". Harsh Narayan, 'The Dharmic outlook in Studies' in *Religion and Change* (ed.) Madhu Sen, Delhi, 1985, p.5; Kane, P.V., *History of Dharamsastra*, Vol.-I, p.1.
20. Zimmer, H., *Philosophies of India*, p.163, as quoted by Organ, T.W., *The Hindu Quest for the Perfection of Man*, p.131.
22. According to Van Buitenen, "*dharma* is all that activity that a man if he to live fittingly is required to contribute to the fixed order of things to the norms of the universe, which is good and not to be altered."–Buitenen, J.A.B. Van, *Dharma* and *Moksa* in *Philosophy East and West* (1955); Tripathi, P.V., *op. cit.*,

pp.30-31.

23. *Taittirīya Āraṇayaka*. 10.79.
24. *Mahābhārata*, 12.110-10-11.
25. Kane, P.V., *op. cit.*, p.1.
26. Dasgupta, Surama, *Development of Moral Philosophy in India*, p.5.
27. *Mahābhārata*, Karṇa Parva, 69.57.
28. Ambree, A.T., *Sources of Indian Tradition*, p.215.
29. Sinha, A.K., *Readings in Early Indian Socio-Cultural History*, p.72.
30. Coller, John, M.,. *Dharma*: An expression of Universal order, *Philosophy East and West* 22 (1972), 134.
31. Pandey, R.B., *Bhartiya Niti Ka Vikas*, Patna, 1965, p.40; Creel, Austin, B., *Dharma in Hindu Ethics*, Calcutta, 1977, p.11
32. Keith, A.B., *Religion and Philosophy of the Vedas and the Upanisads*, Harward, 1925, p.249; Saksena, S.K.,. Moral Philosophy of Indiạ in *Studies in the Cultural History of India* (ed.) Metraux, S.G., and Crouzet, F., Agra, 1965, p.409.
33. *Mahābhārata*, *Sāntiparva*, 294.29; Pandey, R.B., *op. cit.*, p.2.
34. Sinha, A.K., *op. cit.*, p.64.
35. For conception of *Ṛta*, See, Hiriyana, M., *Essentials of Indian Philosophy*, pp.150-151; Dasgupta, S.N., *A History of Indian Philosophy*, Delhi, 1976, pp.22,37,72, Nikam, N.A., *Some Concepts of Indian Culture*, Simla, 1973, p.2.
36. "The word *dharma* or *dharman* is used atleast about 60 times in the *Ṛgveda* by itself is not preceded by a particle like *vi* or some words like *satya*." Kane, P.V., *History of Dharamsastra*, Vol. I, p.1.
37. "The shape of *dharma* is developed from *Ṛta*"-Tripathi, Harihar Nath, *Pracina Bharat mein Rajya aur Nyayapalika*, pp.5-6.
38. Creel, A.B., *op. cit.*, p.10; Pandey, R.B., *op. cit.*, p.40, Bose, Avinash Chandra, *Hymns from the Vedas*, Bombay, 1966, pp. 7-8.
39. Nikam, N.A., *op. cit.*, pp.2-3; Crawford, S., Cromwell, *Evolution of Hindu Ethical Ideals*, Calcutta, 1974, pp.3-4 ff.
40. Das, Bhagwan, *The Science of Social Organisation*, Vol.-I, Madras, 1950, pp.49-50; Organ, T.W., *The Hindu Quest for the Perfection of Man*, Ohio, 1970, p.212.

41. Agarwal, V.S., *Veda-Vidya*, pp.186-87.
42. Keith, A.B., *Encyclopedia of Religion and Ethics*, (ed.) J. Hastings, Vol. I; Zimmerman. R., 'The Evidences of RK-Texts for the Meaning of Rta' in *Proceedings of All India Oriental Conference*, 5th session, Vol.-I, Lahore, 1930, p.216.
    In this meaning *Ṛta* bears a resemblance with *Arsa* of *Avesta*- used for denoting the unalterable, and divine order of creation. Loui Reno holds that before coming to India Aryans held some views regarding the notion of '*rta*' as evident by the synonomous *Arsa* of *Avesta*. See, Mills, Lorens (ed.) Avesta, Yarun as quoted by Ranjit Singh, *Dharma Kei Hindu Avadharana*, Allahabad, 1977, pp.35-36; Reno, L., *Vedic India*, London, 1889, p.56.
43. Nikam, N.A., *op. cit.*, p,2; Singh, Ranjit, *op. cit.*, pp.35-36.
44. *Ṛgveda*, 10.2.8; 1.23.5; Crowford, S., Cromwell, *op cit*, pp.10-11.
45. Sinha, H.N., *Sovereignity in Ancient Indian Polity*, London, 1936, p.4; *Rgvedic Studies* (Series III), Time, M., Sundar Raj, 1983, Madras, pp.37-38.
46. *Ṛgveda*, 1.2.8, 1.65.3-4.
47. *Ibid*, 5.63.7.
48. Hindery, R., *op. cit.*, pp.50-52.
49. See, *Ṛgveda*, 10.67.20; 9.75.2; 7.34.8.
50. Pandey, R.B., *op. cit.*, pp.45-47.
51. *Encyclopedia of Religion and Ethics*, Vol. IV, (ed.) J. Hastings, New York. (The article of Jolly on Religion)
52. Zimmerman, R.,.The evidence of the RK-Text for the meaning of Rtạ in *Proceedings of All India Oriental Conference*, Vol.-I, Lahore, 1926, p.216, as quoted, Sinha, A.K., *op. cit.*, p.68.
53. For relation between, *rta*, *satya* and *dharma*, see, Sen, Madhu, *Studies in Religion and Change*, New Delhi. 1983, p.23; Tripathi,, Harihar Nath, *op. cit.*, p.5.
54. *Ṛgveda*, 10.190.1; Upadhyaya, Baldeva, *Bhartiya Darsana*, p.22; Pandey, R.B., *op. cit.*, p.39; Velkar, H.D., 'Rta and Satya in *Ṛgveda*' in *Proceedings and Transctions of All India Oriental Conference*, 20th session, Bhuvnesvara, Vol.-II, Part-I, p.3.
55. Organ, T.W., *The Quest for the Perfection of Man*, Athens, 1970, p.211; Bhagwan Das, *The Science of Social Organizations*, Madras, 1970, p.49ff.

56. *Taittirīya Upaniṣad*, 1.11.
57. *Brhadaranayaka Upanisad*, 1.4.14; 1.3.28.
58. Vora, D.P., *Evolution of Moral in the Epics*, p.184.
59. For details of general code (*samanya dharma*) see, Pandey R.B., *op. cit.*, pp.8-9.
60. Ayiengar, K.V.R., *Some Aspects of Ancient Indian Polity*, Patna, 1988, pp.89-90; For *sadharana* and *visista dharma*, see Johari, Manorama, *Ethics and Politics in Ancient India*, Varanasi, 1918, p.77 ff.
61. Pande, G.C., *The Meaning and Process of Culture*, Agra, 1972, p.97.
62. Ghokhale, B.G., *Indian Thought Through the Ages*, Bombay, 1961, p.25; Gopal, Lallanji& Yadav, B.N.S., *Bhartiya Samskrti*, Gorakhpur, 1962, p.26.
63. Radhakrishnan, S., *Religion and Society*, 1966, p.104.
64. In the Vedic literature, due to excess of passages dealing with rituals, there left a very few space for moral virtues though, there are not totally absent.
65. The spiritualistic outlook of philosophy of the Upaniṣads plays important role in revealing the moral aspect of *dharma*. See- *Bṛhadāraṇayaka Upaniṣad*, 1.4.2.3; *Chāndogya Upaniṣad*, 1.12.2.5.
66. *Sāntiparva*, 34.103, 62.10-11, 149.33, 204.7-10.
67. *Ibid*, 156.3-5. Similar, opinions are also expressed in the *Rāmāyana*, Ayodhya kand, 101-10-14; Vora, D.P., *op. cit.*, p.218.
68. *Manusmṛti*, VI-218.
69. *Yājñavalkyasmrti*, 1/22.
70. *Bhāgvata Purāṇa*, 7-11.5-12.
71. *Āpastamba Dharmasūtra*, II. 20.22.23.
72. *Mahābhārata*, *Sāntiparva*, 167. 8-9. *Udyoga Parva*, 124.34-38.
73. *Droṇa Parva*, 15.1.37.
74. *Yājñavalkyasmrti*, I. 115.
75. *Arthaśāstra*, 1-7.
76. *Kāmasūtra*, 1.2.7-15.
77. *Ṛgveda*, X. 129.4.
78. *Atharvaveda*, IX. 2.
79. *Ṛgveda*, IX 113.11.

80. Gupta, S.N., *op. cit.*, pp.38-39.
81. Devraj, N.K., *The Mind and Spirit of India*, p.81.
82. *ibid*, pp.81-82.
83. Ayer, P.S.S., *op. cit.*, p.152.
84. *Mahābhārata, Vanaparva*, 33.37-38; Pandey, R.B., *op. cit.*, p.29.
85. Tripathi, P.V., *op. cit.*, p.291.
86. *Bhāgvata Purāṇa*, 3.26,27.
87. For details see, Tripathi, P.V., *op. cit.*, pp.289-293.
88. *Māhabhārata, Vana parva*, 33.30.
89. *Bhagvata Gītā*, 7.11.
90. *Rāmāyaṇa*, 329.5.
91. *Arthaśāstra*, 1.7.
92. *Kāmasūtra*, 2.11.
93. Gupta, S.N., *op. cit.*, p.79
94. *Ṛgveda*, 10.129; Damodaran, K., *Bharitya Cintana Parampara*, pp. 40-41.
95. Sinha, A.K., *op. cit.*, p.20.
96. Dessun, P., *Philosophy of the Upanisads*, (Eng. Tr., by A.S. Gaden,) pp.2-3; as quoted by Hiriyana, M., *Outlines of Indian Philosophy*, p.47 ; Mukherjee, R.K., *Hindu Civilization*, p.133.
97. The dialogue between *Yama* and *Naciketā*, *Maitriyi* and *Yājñavalkya* in the *Kath* and *Bṛhadāraṇyaka Upaniṣad* respectively may be taken as instances of this feeling that worldly pleasures can not be the cannot be the ultimate goal of man. *Kathopanisad*, 1.2.1; *Bṛhadāraṇyaka Upaniṣad*, 4.6.
98. *Bṛhadāraṇyaka Upaniṣad*,
99. *Chāndogya Upaniṣad*, 7-22-1
100. Sinha, A.K., *Dimensions of Indian History*, New Delhi, 2004, p.45
101. Verma, Jaya, *op. cit.*, p.79.
102. *Sarva Darsan Samgrah*, p.4; Pande, G.C., *Mulya Mimamsa*, p.101.
103. Hiriyana, M., *op. cit.*, p.10; Pandey, R.B., *op. cit.*, pp.87-89.
104. Dutta, D., & Chatterjee, S., *An Introduction to Indian Philosophy*, p.66; Devraja, N.K., *The Mind and Spirit of India*, pp.89-91.
105. Devraja, N.K., *op. cit.*, p.89.

106. *Kamasutra*, I.2.
107. Chattopadhyay, D.D., *Lokayata*, p.63, as quoted by Damodaran, K., *Bhartiya Cintana Parampara*, p.85.
108. *Yojsastra*, 1.52.
109. *Udana Jatyandha Varga*, 8.
110. *Bhagwad Gītā*, 7.11.
111. *Bhagwad Gītā*, 3.13.
112. Pandey, R.B., *op. cit.*, p.6.
113. Dasgupta, S.N., *Yoga Philosophy in Relation to Other Systems of Indian Thought*, p.316.
114. Organ, T.W., *op. cit.*, p.22.
115. Hiriyana, M., *op. cit.*, p.266.
116. Lad, A.K., *A Comparative Study of the Concept of Liberation in Indian Philosophy*, Rewa, 1967, p.2.
117. Ayer, P.S.S., *op. cit.*, p.153.
118. *Kathopaniṣad*, 3.14.
119. Kane, P.V., *op. cit.*, pp.363-64, Williams, M., *Sanskrit-English Dictionary*.
120. *Bṛhadāraṇayaka Upaniṣad*. III 1,5.
121. *ibid*, 4.4,7.
122. Dutta & Chatterjee, *An Introduction to Indian Philosophy*, p.18.
123. *Nyaya bhasya*, 1.19.
124. Verma, Jaya, *op. cit.*, p.108.
125. *Nyāya Sūtra*, I.2.
126. Ayer, P.S.S., *op. cit.*, p.151.
127. *Bṛhadāraṇayaka Upaniṣad*, 2.5.19; Ranade, R.D., *A Constructive Survey of Upanisadic Philosophy*, Bombay, 1968, pp.221-222; Hiriyana, M., *Outlines of Indian Philosophy*, pp.55-56; Dasgupta, S.N., *A History of Indian Philosophy*, Vol-1, Delhi, 1976, pp. 27, 47-48.
128. The well-known sayings like, *Tattvamasi*, *aham Brahmasmi*, and emphasis on *atmanam viddhi*, in the *Upaniṣads* are enough to show this development. See, Aurobindo, *The Foundations of Indian Culture*, Pondichery, 1959, p.114; Hiriyana, M., *Essentials of Indian Philosophy*, London, 1956, pp.21-28.
129. The difference between knowledge and wisdom can be explained through the difference between *Aparā* and *Parāvidyā*.

Aparāvidyā has been defined as that knowledge through which one can achieve only worldly things while through *parāvidyā amartattva*, immortality or *mokṣa* can be attained. -*Muṇḍaka Upaniṣad*, I, 1.4.5.

130. Ayer, P.S.S., *op. cit.*, p.153.

5. Conclusion

As 'History' is the study of human activities in the past and 'Value' is the natural instinct of human nature that manifests itself at the different levels of human consciousness from the lowest to the highest through the satisfaction that is attained by the fulfillment of the need, want or desire of a human person.[1] Thus, both these terms possess a close relationship with each other and can be understood only with a reference to the human person.[2] If, on the one hand, human activity and past consciousness play an important role in the notion of history,[3] on the other hand, human nature can be regarded as the determinant factor for defining the term 'value'.[4] Human person, thus, occupies the prime position in both concepts. Due to the centrality of man in both concepts, viz. 'history' and 'value' scholars have no unanimity regarding their scope and definitions.[5] Scholars have been adopted the various approaches to define these notions. If history has been defined from scientific[6] and psychological[7] points of view, value has been defined on utilitarian, philosophical and moral principles.[7A] The followers of the scientific approach consider history a science through developing an objective approach[8] and the followers of the philosophical approach declare history, a philosophy through developing a subjective approach[9] but the followers of both approaches have committed the uni-lateral fallacy and fail to analyze history as 'History' only. History is both science[10] and philosophy[11] but primarily it is 'history' and the history alone. In fact both these approaches are 'tools' that can be used to express the nature of the history.[12] Thus history is created from the co-ordination of both the approaches.[13] Its scientific approach is essential for the factual and objective analysis of the events,[14] then philosophical approach is equally important for the explanatory description of fact presented through the scientific analysis.

Value, on the other hand, is related deeply to the human nature and can be defined only with reference to it.[15] All those things that give man satisfaction through fulfilling his needs, wants, desires and are concerned with the growth, development, enhancement and satisfaction of human person possess value.[16] Man, thus, seeks values in the natural way from the lowest to the highest depending on his taste, will and desires[17] and this capability of value-seeking transforms him into a moral, social, and finally of cultural being. Culture, can be defined as the totality of values.[18] In wider perspective, therefore, any human activity, thought or idea, feeling, sentiment or emotion, which can promote self-development of the individual in all its dimensions, can be taken to constitute a value. If the man is a value conscious being and culture is the value seeking, then "history is the process through which the stages of this value seeking are made known to the coming generations of value-seekers." Man plays an important role in the development of both the history and culture, which achieve their fulfillment in the fulfillment of man.

Fact[19] and truth[20] are the two points of history[21] which assign the study of human activities in the past valuational ground. In this way in its process of analyzing human activities history enters in the realm of value. Therefore, the notion of history as history of ideas[22] presented by Collingwood transformed history into the history of value.

Because in the wider perspective culture is nothing but the continuation of values, history of human culture remains nothing but the history of values.[23]

As already stated, in ancient Indian perspective the notion of value has been manifested through the notion of *Purūṣārtha Catuṣṭay*[24] which is the co-ordination of the different values of life. Values that are coordinated in this system were prevalent in Indian culture from an early age but they lacked clear-cut theoretical conception[25] and as they were not inter-related, the importance of their mutual dependence was also not known. Therefore, the most important characteristic of the Indian value system, developed in the form of *Purūṣārtha-Catuṣṭay*, is that through it every value of life was accorded a position according to its respective importance in the human life. Another idea that is reflected from this coordination is their relative importance in human life. It gives a message that every value of life is important whether biological or spiritual and without achieving lower level, higher level cannot be achieved. It is not possible to reach the highest level without passing through the lowest one.[26]

The term '*artha*' in its various connotations includes all the meanings of the objects, means of human pursuit as well as the needs and desires suggesting these pursuits.[27] As used in Indian literature, it means all the things that a man can amass, possess, share, enjoy, lost and destroy.[28] Thus *artha* is both desire and 'to be desire'. Whatever is desired or desirable is meaningful hence 's*arthaka*' and its contrary is '*nirarthaka*', the meaningless or disvalue.[29] As all values are human values,[30] these terms can be valued only in terms of the needs, wants and demands of human life.[31] In the Indian tradition all those things that a man can desire for fulfilling his needs, wants, and demands are included in the broad framework of *Purūṣārtha*.[32] (Purūṣa=man, *artha*=desire)] i.e. desired by purūṣa of human being. What a man can desire at the most *is Paramārtha*, the highest *artha* meaning ultimate end or *summum bonum.*[33] In this connotation *artha* possess a resemblance with the concept of good developed in the Greek culture.[34] 'Good', as Aristotle defines, is that which every one aims at.[35] *Artha* and 'Good', therefore, are two aspects of the same concept of value. Every value either extrinsic or intrinsic is *artha* as manifested through term '*artha*' in the word *Purūṣārtha.*[36] Thus, *artha* primarily meant value but in the notion of the *Purūṣārtha-Catuṣṭay* it was included as material value and in this form its tradition was prevalent in ancient India from an early age. A glance over the Indian history and culture would clearly reveal that India has witnessed many changes in its historical course. Owing to these changes the general mentality and outlook of the ancient Indian people towards life and its priorities changed significantly. This transformation in the attitude of people resulted in the change of point of view regarding the values of life. Ṛgvedic Aryans possessed a positive attitude towards life and its problems, and the values that they praised were material and empirical. The society, depicted in the *Ṛgveda* gave the reflection of the attitude of the early Aryans who were strongly attracted towards the material aspect of life. In the hymns of the *Ṛgveda*, they had demanded all the pursuits of material and empirical pleasure from gods. The desire of wealth, cows, heroic sons, property, constituted the subject-matter of most of the hymns of *Ṛgveda*. Thus it can be said with certainty that Rgvedic Aryans possessed a strong world-affirmative attitude and had no interest, rather knowledge of the world negating thoughts. They possessed strong desires for the worldly pleasures and comforts and the highest goal of their life was to achieve more and more material and empirical pursuits. Though in those days theoretical conception of the word '*artha*' was not developed but in its various usages in *Ṛgveda*[37], it denotes for a general sense of material and empirical value. From this it appears that the threads of theoretical conception as material value of *artha* in *Purūṣārtha*, was initiated in the Rgvedic period. In the later Vedic period no significant changes occurred in the attitude of the people. The prominent change that occurred was the replacement of early Vedic simplicity by complex rituals in the performance of the *Yajñas*, which were the only medium for achieving any goal whether material or empirical. This complexity of ritual and extravagant performance of *Yajñas* gave birth to a thoughtful reaction against them which resulted in the development of the idea of *antaryajña* and *manoyajña*, i.e. performance of *Yajña* on mental and inner level.[38] This developed a spiritualistic philosophy that received its culmination in the philosophy of *Brahman-Ātman-Mokṣa*, in the period of the *Upaniṣads*. The natural declarant of this tendency was the idea of detachment, i.e. detachment from the material world and its possessions. But the spiritualism of *Upaniṣads* did not create hindrance in the development of *artha* consciousness. Rather in the form of *Paramārtha, artha* touches the highest level of human desires, on the material plane the attraction of the people towards material achievement was not ceased in the *Upaniṣads*, and it was presented in the various *Upaniṣads* in its multi dimensional form. Despite of the development of spiritual thinking, the importance of *artha* in totality of material achievements remained continues. The spiritualistic thoughts of *Upaniṣads* and sects of heterodox tradition, namely Buddhist and Jain, gave birth to the attitude of renunciation (*Nivṛtti*) of world that had emphasis on the attainment of *mokṣa*. Due to non-practical view of this philosophy against it two types of reactions developed. In opposition of strong *nivṛttimārga*, the Cārāvakas developed strong *pṛavatimārga*. On the other side with the coordination of *pṛavati* and *nivṛtti* a balanced attitude of life was developed. Cārāvaka philosophy faced severe criticism while the second attitude enhanced the coordination capacity of Indian culture and in spite of taking *mokṣa* as the highest objective, did not discard the importance of *artha* and *kāma*. This attitude was manifested through the notion of *Purūṣārtha-Catuṣṭay* and was developed to a large extent in the periods of Epics.

In the *Māhabhārata* the idea of *artha* was developed in the two forms. In the form of material value and secondly in the form of politics. This tradition of *artha* in the form of politico-economic value received culmination in the *Arthaśāstra* of Kauṭilya that deals primarily with the matters of statecraft and polity. This connotation of *Arthaśāstra* was the result of the merging of two different sciences into one, i.e. of *Vārta* and *Daṇdaniti*.[39] The economic aspect of the life was dealt in ancient India in the science of *Vārta*, and though we not have any available treatise on the subject, it was regarded as an important branch of learning. Even Kauṭilya included it in his description of lores. *Daṇdaniti* deals with the science of polity and state and in wider perspective includes and those things that were important for a state. The tradition of *Daṇdaniti* prevailed in India before Kauṭilya also and the school of Uśanasa regarded it as the only science worthy to be studied.[40] *Arthaśāstra* according to Kauṭilya was the science of polity and statecraft and the tradition of it prevailed prior to Kauṭilyan period also because Kauṭilya gave the names of the promulgators of *Arthaśāstra* and same names were also referred to in the *Śāntiparva* of the *Mahābhārata*. As a class of those who were interested in military and administrative activities and had chosen these activities as their profession, namely *Ksatriyas* was existed in India from Ṛgvedic period. In the collective way duties ascribed to the members of this social group was known as *Kṣātradharma* that included in itself the idea of *Rājdharma* also.[41] It is in sense of *Rājdharma* or duties for the king that we presuppose the existence of some persons, *risis* or thinkers in this context to prepare the code of kingly duties and they may be regarded as the predecessors of Kauṭilya whose heritage were adopted by Kauṭilya and that developed in a more refined form in his text.

In fact the connotation of *artha* as wealth was developed in the post-Kauṭilyan age. Manu followed this meaning.[42] Vātsyāyan also defined *artha* as material possession. In his *Nitiśataka*, Brhathari called *artha* 'vitta' and *Sukra* also followed this tradition. Thus, in Indian tradition in post-Kauṭilyan age *artha* was used prominently to denote economic value.

The tradition of *artha*, as revealed from this study remained prevalent in ancient India from the very early age. *Artha* was regarded as the important value of life. In fact, the tradition of *Arthaśāstra* in ancient Indian value system was the tradition of values, through its connotation never remained the same. Originally and initially it is used in the sense of value and in the historical course various changes occurred in its notion. It though, remained always to be a value, but its scope changed with its changing connotations. In the historical course *artha* and *arthaśāstra* underwent many changes and witnessed gradual shrinkage in its connotations but it always remained the subject of great concern.

NOTES AND REFERENCES

1. Hiriyana, M., *Indian Conception of Values*, p.2.
2. Nikam, N.A., *op. cit.*, p.4.
3. Carr, E.H., *What is History*, London, 1962. (Reprint 1977), p.112.
4. Pande, G.C., *The Meaning and Process of Culture*, p.1; Sinha, A.K. 'Mulya Kei Avadharna aur Swaroop' pp.182-83; Pande, G.C., Mulya Mimansa, pp.74-75.
5. Deveraj, N.K., *Philosophy, Religion, and Culture*, Varanasi, 1974, p.1; Mackenzie, J.S., *A Manual of Ethics*, London, 1929, p.218.

6. Dilthey regarded history more than science but J.B. Bury declares history 'as science no more or less'.
7. Hegel makes the history, philosophy, see, Budhaprakash, *Itihasa Darsana*, Varanasi, 1968, p.170; Pande, G.C., *Itihasa kei Swaroop evam Siddhanta*, pp.5-6.

7A. Bentham, Mill, Sidgewick tries to define the notion of value through Utilitarian Approach. Perry and Hartmann try to define it in terms of interest and essence. See, Gupta Shantinath, *op. cit.*, pp.9-12.

8. 'Historiography and Historical Methodology', *The New Encyclopedia Britannica*, Vol.-8., p.945 and above; Buddha prakash, *op. cit.*, p.3; Pande, G.C., *op. cit.*, p.5; Carr, E.H., *op. cit.*, p.103.
9. Banerjee, N.V., *Concept of Philosophy*, 1968, p.40; Oakshot, M., *Experience and its Modes*, 1933, p.99; Buddha Prakash, *op. cit.*, p.170.
10. For the relation of history and science, see, Carr, E.H. *op. cit.* p.46-71.
11. Philosophy is not mental but theoretical process whose objective is to describe the truth.–see, Banerjee. N.V., *op. cit.*. p.31.
12. Verma, Jaya, *op. cit.*, p.2.
13. Historian establishes a balance between facts find their explanations, fact, and value. These cannot be separated. See, Carr, E.H., p.112
14. *Buddha Prakash*, *op. cit.*, p.3., Carr, E.H., p.103; 'Historiography and Historical methodology', *The New Encyclopedia Britannica*, Vol-8, p.945; Sheikh Ali, B., *History its Theory and Method*, (Reprint), Madras, 1984, p.2-3.
15. Pandey, R.B., *op. cit.*, p.4; Nikam, N.A., *op. cit.*, p.47; Mukherjee, Radha Kamal, *The Social Structure of Values*, Delhi, 1965, pp.4-5. Durant, Will, *The Pleasures of Philosophy*, New York, 1973, pp.76-77.
16. Pandey R.B., *op. cit.*, p.4.
17. Sinha, A.K., *Mulya Kei Avadharna aur Swaroop*, pp.182-183.
18. Pande, G.C., *The Meaning and Process of Culture*, pp.2-3.
19. Sinha, A.K., *Reading in Early Socio-Cultural History*, pp.118-19; "History is a continuous process of action and reaction

between the historian and his fact"—See Carr, E.H., *op. cit.*, p.12.

20. Truth is the word that merges in itself both fact and value—see, Carr, E.H., *op. cit.*, pp.112-113.
21. Walsh, *'Meaning of History'* as quoted by Verma, Jaya, *op. cit.*, p.2.
22. Collingwood, R.G., *The Idea of History*, London, 1973, pp.296-97; 307-308.
23. Carr, E.H., *op. cit.*, p.112.
24. "Value is *Purūṣārtha*" Pande, G.C., Mulya Mimansa, p.259; Hiriyana, M., *op. cit.* p.6, fn., 17.
25. Though words, *Dharma*, *Artha* and *Kāma* are used in the *Ṛgveda* but their theoretical conception was not developed in that age.
27. Zimmer, H., *The Philosophies of India*, p.35.
28. Organ, T.W., *The Hindu Quest for the Perfection of Man*, (Indian edition), 1994, New Delhi, p.122.
29. Sinha, A.K., *op. cit.*, p.49.
30. Nikam, N.A., *op. cit.*, p.47,
31. Pandey, R.B., *op. cit.*, p.4; Hiriyana, M., *op. cit.*, p.2
32. "The mere satisfaction of desires is not, however, value, unless the satisfaction a conscious satisfaction. Conscious satisfaction is enjoyment, while animals merely satisfy their desires, man alone is capable of 'enjoyment', therefore, all values are in a significant sense 'human value', *Purūṣārtha*, the enjoyment of consciously pursued value". see Nikam, N.A., *op. cit.*, p.47, also Gupta, S.N., *op. cit.*, p.15.
33. Sinha, A.K., *op. cit.*, p.49.
34. Maitra, in connection with the mimamsaka's concept of *artha*, uses word 'good' as its synonym, see, Maitra, S.K., *op. cit.*, p.88.
35. Sinha, A.K., *op. cit.*, p.49.
36. Hiriyana used words 'ista' and 'dvista' as *Sanskrt* equivalent of value and disvalue respectively.—Hiriyana, *op. cit.*, p.2.
37. Such as wish, goal, gain, end, wealth, object, purpose, etc as indicated already.
38. Pande, G.C., *Bhartiya Parampara kei Mula Svara*, Delhi, 1981, p.44.

39. Pande, G.C., *Foundations of Indian Culture*, Vol. II, p.153.
40. *Arthaśāstra*, 1.2.2-7; Bhandarkar, D.R., *Some Aspects of Ancient Hindu Polity*, Patna, 1988, p.1.
41. Sinha, A.K., "Dharma, Rajdharma, and the Process of State Formation in Ancient India", *Bharti* (1983) Bulletin of Deptt. of Ancient Indian History, Culture and Archaeology, B.H.U., Varanasi, pp.50-55.
42. *Manusmṛti*, 4.170.

Bibliography

Original Sources :

Agni Purāṇa, Anandasrama, Poona, 1900, (Eng.tr.) M.N. Dutta, Calcutta, 1903.

Aitereya Āraṇayaka, (ed.) A.B. Keith, Oxford, 1909.

Aitereya Brāhmaṇa, with Sayana Commentary, Anandasrama, Poona, 1931; (Eng. tr.) A.B. Keith, Harvard Oriental Series, Vol. 25, Cambridge, 1920.

Amarkośa, with commentary of Mallinath (ed.) A.A. Ramanathan, Madras, 1971.

Āpastamba Dharmasūtra, with the commentary of Hardutta, (ed.) G.Buhler, Bombay Sanskrit series, Poona, 1932.

Arthaśāstra of Kauṭilya, (ed.) R.P. Kangle, Part 1-2, 2nd edition, Bombay, 1963.

Asṭādhayāyi of Panini, Nirnay Sagar Press, 1929.

Atharvaveda, (ed.) R.Roth and W.D. Whitney, Berlin, 1856; with Sayana commentary (ed.) S.P. Pandit, Bombay, 1895-98; (Eng. tr.) W.D. Whitney, Cambridge, 1905; (Eng. tr.) Bloomfield, M., *Sacred Books of the East*, Vol. 42., Oxford, 1897.

Bauddhāyana *Dharmasūtra* with Govind Swami Commentary, (ed.) A.C. Sastri, Varanasi, 1934; (Eng. Tr.); G. Buhler, *Scared Books of the East*, Vol. 2, Oxford, 1897.

Bhagwadgītā, Geeta Press Edition, Gorakhpur, 1933.

Brahmānda Purana, (Venketesvara Press edition) Bombay, 1931.

Bṛhadāraṇayaka Upaniṣad, (ed. tr.) S. Radhakrishnan, IVth

impression, London, 1974; Geeta Press edition, Gorakhpur.

Chāndogya Upaniṣad, Geeta Press Edition, Gorakhpur, 1952.

Gautama Dharmasūtra, with Haridutta's Commentary, (ed.) G. Sastri, Anandasarma, Poona, 1931; (Eng. tr.) G. Buhler, *Scared Books of the East*, Vol-2, Oxford, 1897.

Iśa Upaniṣad, Geeta Press Edition, Gorakhpur, 1952.

Kāmandakiya Nitisāra, (ed.) T. Ganapati Sastri, Trivendrum, 1912.

Kāmasūtra of Vātsayāyan, Chokhamba Series, Varanasi.

Kathopaniṣad, Gita Press Edition, Gorakhpur, 1952.

Mahābhārata with Nilkantha Commentary, (ed.) R. Kinjvadekar, Poona, 1926-33; B.O.R.I edition (ed.) V.S. Sautharkar and others, Poona, 1927-66; (Eng.tr.) M.N. Dutta, Calcutta, 1895-1905; Geeta Press edition (with Hindi tr.) Gorakhpur, 1968.

Mahābhāshya of Patanjali, (ed.) F. Keilhorn, Bombay.

Maitrayani Upaniṣad, Geeta Press, Gorakhpur, 1952.

Manusmṛti with Kulluka Bhatta commentary, (ed.) Gopal Sastri Nene; (Eng.tr.) A.C. Barnell & E.W. Hopkins, London, 1884 (reprint) Ludhiyana, 1972, Vol. 25, Oxford, 1886; (Hindi tr.) Hargovinda Sastri, Varanasi, 1970.

Muṇḍaka Upaniṣad, Gita Press edition, Gorakhpur, 1952.

Nighantu and Nirukta, (ed.) Laksman Saroop, Delhi, 1967.

Nitiśataka, Venketeshvara Press, Bombay; Chokhamba Sanskrit Series, Varanasi, 1981.4.

Nitivakyamrta, (ed.) P.L. Soni, Bombay, 1921.

Praśana Upaniṣad, Geeta Press, Gorakhpur, 1952.

Radhakrishnan, S., *The Principal Upanisads*, London, 1953.

Ṛgveda, (ed.) Vedic Samsodhana Mandal, Poona, 1933, Vol. 1-4; with Sayana commentary, (ed.) Laksman Saroop, Vol. 1-4, Varanasi, 1939; (Eng. tr.) R.T.H. Grifith (Reprint) Delhi, 1976.

Sāmaveda with Sayana Commentary, Anandasarma, Poona.

Śatpath Brāhmaṇa, (ed.) A Weber, London, 1885; with Sayana commentary (Eng. tr.) Jullius Engling, *Scared Books of East*, Vol.44 (reprint) Delhi, 1972.

Śukla Yajurveda, Chokhama Series, Banaras.

Śvetāśvatara Upaniṣad, Gita Press edition, Gorakhpur, 1922.

Taittirīya Āraṇayaka, with Sayana Commentry, Anandasrama Granthavalli, Poona, 1897-1898.

Taittirīya Brāhmaṇa, (ed.) H. N. Apte, Anandasrama, Poona, 1898; (Eng. tr.) A. B. Keith, Harvard Oriental Series, Vol. 18, Cambridge.

Taittirīya Upaniṣad, Geeta Press, Gorakhpur.

Vālmiki Rāmāyaṇa, (ed.) P. L. Vaidya, Baroda, 1960-71; (Eng. tr.) M.N. Dutta, Calcutta, 1892-94.

Vāyu Purāṇa, Venketesvara Press edition, Bombay, 1933; (ed.) Sriram Acarya, Bareilly, 1969.

Yājñavalkya Smṛti, (ed. & tr.) V.N., Mandalik, Bombay, 1980; with Mitaksara Commentary, (ed.) J.R. Gharpure, Bombay, 1919; (Hindi; tr.) U.C. Pandey Varanasi, 1977.

Secondary Sources:

Agarwal, V. S., *India as known to Panini*, Lucknow, 1952.

Altekar, A. S., *State and Government in Ancient India*, (reprint) Delhi, 1984.

Anand, S., *Ksatriyas in Ancient India*, Delhi, 1985.

Arora, U.P.,(ed.) *Graco-Indica-Demetrius Galanos Memorial Volume*, Delhi, 1988.

Atreya, B.L., *Bhartiya Nitisastra Ka Itihasa*, Lucknow, 1964.

Ayengar, K.V.R., *Some Aspects of Hindu View of Life According to Dharmsastra*, Baroda, 1952.

—*Some Aspects of Ancient Indian Polity*, Patna, 1988.

Ayer, P.S.S., *The Evolution of Hindu Moral Ideals*, (reprint) Delhi, 1976.

Bandopadhyaya, N.C., *Development of Hindu Polity and Political Theories*, (reprint), Calcutta, 1927.

Banerjee, N.V., *Spirit of Indian Philosophy*, Delhi, 1974.

Barua, B.M., *A History of Pre-Buddhist Indian Philosophy*, Calcutta, 1921.

Basham, A.L., *The Wonder that was India*, Delhi, 1978.

Basu, J., *India of the Age of the Brahmanas*, Calcutta, 1969.

Bhandarkar, D.R.,—*Some Aspects of Ancient Hindu Polity*, Patna, 1988.

Bloomfield, M., *The Religion of the Vedas*, Delhi, 1972.

Bose, A.C., *Hymns from the Vedas*, Bombay, 1967.

Buddha Prakash, *Itihas Darsana*, Varanasi, 1961.

Carr, E.H., *What is History?* London, 1961, (reprint 1977).

Charkraborti, H.P., *Vedic India, Political and Legal Institutions in Vedic Literature*, Calcutta, 1981.

Chattopadhyay, K., *Studies in the Vedic and Indo-Iranian Religion and Literature* (ed.) V.N. Mishra, Delhi, 1977.

Clayton, A.C., *The Ṛgveda and the Vedic Religion*, (reprint), Delhi, 1984.

Collingwood, R.G., *The Idea of History*, London, 1973.

Commarswami, A.K., *Spiritual Authority and Temporal Power in the Indian Theory of Government*, Delhi,1978.

Crawford, S. C., *The Evolution of Hindu Moral Ideals*, Calcutta, 1974.

Creel, A. B., *Dharma in Hindu Ethics*, Calcutta, 1977.

Dandekar, R. N., *Insights into Hinduism*, Delhi, 1979 .

Das, Bhagwan., *The Science of Social Organisation*, Vol. 1., Madras, 1910.

—*Purūṣārtha*, Varanasi, 1966.

Dasgupta, Surama, *Development of Moral Philosophy in India*, Bombay, 1978.

Dasgupta, S.N., *A History of Indian Philosophy*, Vol. 1, (reprint.) Delhi, 1976.

Deshmukh, P.R., *Indus Civilization, Ṛgveda and the Hindu Culture*, Nagpur, 1982.

Deveraja, N.K., *Philosophy, Religion & Culture*, Varanasi, 1975

—*Samskriti Ka Darsanika Vivecana*, Lucknow, 1972.

—*The Mind and Spirit of India*, Delhi, 1967.

—*Bhartiya Sanskriti*, Lucknow, 1990

Dikshitar, V.R.R., *The Mauryan Polity*, Madras, 1932.

Drekmeier, C., *Kingship and Community in Early India*, Stanford University Press, California, 1987.

Durant, Will, *Our Oriental Heritage*, New York, 1954.

—*The Pleasures of Philosophy*, New York, 1973

Embree, A.T., *Sources of Indian Tradition*, Indian edition, 1992.

Ghosal, U. N., *The History of Indian Political Ideas*, Bombay, 1929.

Ghosh, R.C., *History of Hindu Civilization* (reprint) Delhi, 1985.

Ghurye, G. S., *Vedic India*, Bombay, 1979.

Gokhale, B. G., *Ancient India—History & Culture* (reprint) Bombay, 1970.

—*Indian Thought Through the Ages*, Bombay 1961.

Gopal, Lallanji, and Yadav, B.N.S., *Bhartiya Sanskriti*, Gorakhpur, 1962.

Gopal, Lallanji, *Pracina Bhartiya Rajanatik Vicaradhara*, Varanasi, 1999.

Gupta, N.L., (ed.) *Education and Value in Mahabharata*, New Delhi, 1995.

Gupta, Shantinath, *The Indian Concept of Values*, Delhi, 1978.

Hicks, J.H., *Philosophy of Religion*, Delhi 1979.

Hindrey, Roderick, *Comparative Ethics in Hindu and Buddhist Traditions*, Delhi 1978.

Hiriyana, M., *Essentials of Indian Philosophy*, London 1956.

—*Outlines of Indian Philosophy*, (Hindi tr.) Delhi, 1973.

—*Indian Conception of Value*, Mysore, 1975.

Hopkins, E.W., *The Social and Military Position of the Ruling Castes in Ancient India*, Varanasi, 1972,

—*Ethics of India*, New Heaven, 1924.

Jayaswal, K.P., *Hindu Polity*, Part I-II, Banglore, 1943.

Kane, P.V., *History of Dharmasastra*, Vol. I-V, Bhandarkar Oriental Research Institute, Pune, 1968.

Keith, A.B. & Macdonell A.A., *Vedic Index*, Delhi, 1967.

Keith, A.B., *Religion and Philosophy of the Vedas and the Upanisads*, Harward, 1925.

Kosambi, D.D., *An Introduction to Indian History*, Bombay, 1975.

—*The Culture and Civilization of Ancient India in Historical Outlines* (Hindi tr.), Delhi, 1977.

Kunhanraja, C., *The Vedas*, Waltair, 1957.

Law, N.N., *Studies in Ancient Hindu Polity*, Delhi 1975.
MacDonald, K.S., *The Brahmanas of the Vedas*, Delhi, 1979.
Mackenzie, J.S., *A Manual of Ethics*, London, 1929.
Mahadevan, T.M.P., *Outlines of Hinduism*, Delhi, 1984.
Maitra, S.K., *The Ethics of the Hindus*, Calcutta, 1963.
Majumdar, R.C., (ed.) *The Vedic Age*, Bombay, 1971.
—*Ancient India*, Delhi, 1977
Metraux, S.G., & Crouzct, F., (ed.) *Studies in the Cultural History of India*, Agra, 1965.
Mishra, S.C., *Evolution of Kauṭilya's Arthaśāstra*, New Delhi, 1997.
Mittal, K.K., *Materialism in Indian Thought*, 1974
Mukherjee, Radha Kamal, *Indian Scheme of Life*, Bombay, 1951.
—*The Social Structure of Values*, Delhi, 1965.
—*The Destiny of Civilization*, Bombay, 1964.
—*The Dimension of Value*, New Delhi, 2005.
—*The Dynamics of Morals*, New Delhi, 2005.
Mukherjee, RadhaKumud, *Hindu Civilization*, Delhi, 1975.
Murty, K. Sachidananda,*The Indian Spirit*, Waltair, 1965.
Nikam, N.A., *Some Concepts of Indian Culture*, Simla, 1973.
Nilakanta Sastri, K.A., *Age of the Nandas and the Mauryas*, Benaras, 1952.
Organ, T.W., *The Hindu Quest for the Perfection of Man*, Athens, 1970.
Pande, G.C., *Baudha Dharma Kei Vikas Ka Itihasa*, Lucknow, 1963.
—*Studies in the Origin of Buddhism*, Allahabad, 1957.
—*Bhartiya Parampara Kei Mula Svara*, Delhi, 1981.
—*Foundations of Indian Culture*, Vol. I-II, Delhi, 1984.
—*Itihasa, Svarup evam Siddantha*, Jaipur, 1973.
—Consciousness Value Culture, Allahabad, 2006.
—*Mulya Mimamsa*, Jaipur, 1973.
—*The Meaning & Process of Culture*, Agra, 1972.
—*An Approach to Indian Culture and Civilization*, Varanasi, 1985.
Pandey, Rajbali, *Bhartiya Niti Ka Vikas*, Patna, 1962.

Pant, A.D., *A Critical Study of the Arthaśāstra Tradition* (Unpublished D. litt. thesis), Allahabad, 1966.

Pavgee, N.B., *Self-Government in India—Vedic and Post Vedic*, Delhi, 1980.

Prasad, Beni, *Theory of Government in Ancient India*, Allahabad, 1974.

Radha Krishnan S. & Raju, P.T. (ed.) *The Concept of Man*, London, 1966.

Radha Krishnan, S., *Indian Philosophy*, Vol. I-II, London, 1931.

—*The Spirit of Religion*, Delhi, 1978.

—*An Idealist View of Life* (Indian edition) 2000.

—*Eastern Religion and Western Thought*, (Indian edition) 2000.

Ragozin, Z. A., *Vedic India*, Delhi, 1961.

Rao, V.B., *Uttar Vedic Samaja evam Sanskrtri : Ek Adhyayana*, Varanasi, 1966.

Rapson, E. J., *The Cambridge History of India*, Vol. 1, (reprint) Delhi, 1968.

Roy, B.P., *Later Vedic Economy*, Patna, 1984.

Roychowdhary, H.C., (ed.) *History & Culture of Indian People*, Bombay.

—*Political History of Ancient India*, Calcutta, 1972.

Sabine, G.H., *A History of Political Theory*, Indian edition, Calcutta, 1968.

Samadhar, J.N., *Lectures on the Economic Condition of Ancient India*, Patna 1984.

Sathe, S.G., *Moral Choice and Early Hindu Thought* Bombay, 1970.

Sharma, R.S., *Aspects of Political Ideas and Institutions in Ancient India*, Delhi, 1968.

Sharma, U.C., *The Dasarajña War*, Aligarh, 1985.

Sheikh Ali. B., *History : Its Theory and Method* (reprint), Madras, 1984.

Singh, Ranjit, *Dharma Kei Hindu Avadharana*, Allahabad, 1977.

Sinha, A.K., *Shantiparva Mein Visleshit Naitika Vicara*, Allahabad, 1985.

—*Pracina Bharatiya Vaiyaktika evam Samajik Mulayabodh*, Allahabad. 1980.

—*Readings in Early Indian Socio-Cultural History*, New Delhi, 2000.

—*Time Materialism and History*, New Delhi, 2002.

—*Itihasa, Mulya aur Artha*, New Delhi, 2003.

Smith, V.A., The Early History of India (Second edition) Oxford, 1908.

Thapar, Romilla, Asoka and Decline of the Mauryas Delhi, 1977.

—From Lineage to State, Delhi, 1984.

—History of India, Calcutta,

Tripathi, P.V., *Purūṣārtha-Catuṣṭay*, Varanasi, 1970.

Urban, W. M., *Fundamental of Ethics*, New York, 1930.

Varma, V.P., *Studies in Hindu Political Thought and its Metaphysical Foundations*, Varanasi, 1969.

Verma, Jaya, *Pracina Bharat mein Mulya Cetna aur Artha*, New Delhi, 2001

Vora, D.P., *Evolution of Morals in the Epics*, Bombay, 1966.

Williams, M., *Religious Thought and Life in Ancient India*, Calcutta, 1978.

Zimmer. H., *Philosophies of India* (ed.) by J. Campbell, New York, 1963.

Dictionary & Encyclopedias:

A Dictionary of Philosophy (ed.) D.D. Runes, London 1945.

A Dictionary of Philosophy (ed.) M. Rozenthal & P. Udi.

Cambridge Dictionary of Philosophy (Gen Ed.) Robert Audi.

Chambers Twentieth Century Dictionary.

Encyclopedia Americana.

Encyclopedia Britannica, Vol. 1-18, 15th Edition.

Encyclopedia of Religion & Ethics.

Everyman's Encyclopedia.

Hindu Dharma Kosa (ed.) Rajbali Pandey.

International Encyclopedia of Social Sciences.

Oxford Advanced Learner, English Dictionary (New Edition).

Sanskrit-English Dictionary, Moneir Williams.

Sanskrit-English Dictionary, V.S. Apte.
Webster's New World Dictionary, Modern Desk Edition, A Pitamber Simon and Schuster publication, 1999.

Journals, Periodicals and Proceeding, etc.:

Annals of Bhandarkar Oriental Research Institute, Poona.
Bharti,
Contribution to Indian Sociology.
Ethics
Indian Antiquary.
Indian Culture.
Indian Historical Quarterly.
Indian Historical Review.
Journal of American Oriental Society.
Journal of Bihar and Orissa Research Society.
Journal of G.N. Jha Kendriya Sanskrit Vidyapeeth.
Journal of Ideas.
Journal of Indian History.
Journal of Oriental Research.
Journal of the University of Bombay.
Journal of U.P. Historical Society.
Parāmarśa.
Philosophy : East and West.
Prāchya-Pratibhā.
Proceedings and Transactions of Oriental Conferences.
Proceedings of Indian History Congress.
Proceedings of U.P. History Congress.
Purāṇam.
Puravrtta.
Studies in Comparative History and Religion.
U.P. Historical Review.
University of Allahabad Studies.
Yavanika.

Index